The Skills of Teaching: Teaching Delivery Skills

TABLE OF CONTENTS

continued on next page

CHAPTER 6 — EXAMINING THE SKILLS OF TEACHING DELIVERY

The Skills of Teaching:

Teaching Delivery Skills

Sally R. Berenson, M.S. Ed.
David H. Berenson, Ph.D.
Robert R. Carkhuff, Ph.D.

CARKHUFF INSTITUTE of HUMAN TECHNOLOGY

Human Resource Development Press

Publishers of Human Technology

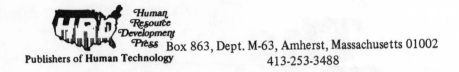

Publishers of Human Technology   Box 863, Dept. M-63, Amherst, Massachusetts 01002
413-253-3488

International Standard Book Number: 0-914234-23-4
Library of Congress Number: 77-091639
First Printing — January, 1979

Designed and Illustrated by Tom Capolongo

ABOUT THE AUTHORS

Sally R. Berenson, M.S. Ed. is Research Associate in Educational Technology, Carkhuff Institute of Human Technology. She has specialized in curriculum development and has been an elementary and secondary teacher for more than ten years. She has instructed teachers in content development skills at all levels of pre-service and in-service teacher training and is a collaborator on the series, **The Do's and Don'ts of Teaching.**

Dr. David H. Berenson is Director of Educational Technology, Carkhuff Institute of Human Technology. He specializes in teacher training and educational administration. A teacher for more than 15 years on elementary and secondary grade levels, Dr. Berenson has spent the last 10 years revolutionizing pre-service and in-service teacher training programs. He has conducted pathfinding research in the development of effective educational delivery systems. Dr. Berenson is co-author of the entire **Skills of Teaching** series.

Dr. Robert R. Carkhuff is Chairman, Carkhuff Institute of Human Technology. He has devoted his life to research and teaching. The author of more than two dozen books on helping and teaching effectiveness, Dr. Carkhuff is internationally renowned as the most-cited reference in the last decade of counseling psychology. A teacher at primary, secondary and post-secondary levels, he continues to coach youth baseball, basketball and football. Dr. Carkhuff is the developer of the human and educational resources development models upon which **The Skills of Teaching** series is based.

The Authors and Their Teachers

This book, like the series it is a part of, is dedicated to the devoted teachers — often forgotten, yet burdened with the greatest responsibilities in the history of humankind. It is to these teachers that we offer a distillation of our efforts in nearly two decades of research into the effective ingredients of learning.

The Skills of Teaching: Teaching Delivery Skills has been written for both education students and teachers already employed in schools. It is designed to overview the skills these students and teachers need to make a delivery to their classes. Included are **lesson preparation skills, diagnostic skills, goal setting skills,** and **reinforcement skills.** Each of these skills is first presented to the reader in an anecdotal form. The reader will follow a first-year teacher through the preparation for and delivery to a class. These anecdotes will serve to illustrate and introduce the skills in an entertaining way. The reader will then be told how to perform the skills and will even be provided with an opportunity to practice the skills.

Where relevant, the reader will be directed to a more in-depth treatment of each skill to be found in the other texts in this series: **Interpersonal Skills, Content Development Skills,** and **Lesson Planning Skills.** This volume will prepare the reader for this more detailed study and serve as a review of the key components of effective teaching delivery.

January, 1979
Amherst, Massachusetts

S.R.B.
D.H.B.
R.R.C.

FOREWORD

The magnitude of the educational enterprise in the United States makes it easy to think of schools as mass production factories and teaching as an impersonal process in shaping students into standardized forms. The development of new technologies has stimulated many persons to imagine learning situations in which teachers play a minor role or are not needed at all. These Orwellian images overlook the tremendous need of human beings, particularly the young, for human encouragement, for close contact with attractive persons whose examples evoke emulation. The young yearn to be with people who care. They are not satisfied with impersonal advice and guidance, nor are they satisfied with casual contacts.

These needs are the central dynamics of complex human learning. Education in all its aspects is a human enterprise. Teaching is an interpersonal activity. Modern technologies provide useful tools for teachers but cannot be substitutes for them. The authors of the **Skills of Teaching** have recognized that teachers and those preparing to teach need not only reaffirmation of the importance of interpersonal skills in teaching but they also need suggestions for integrating these skills with the development of content to teach and the formulation of plans for instructional activities.

Most books about teaching either devote almost sole attention to the content and teaching strategies or they deal with interpersonal relations in the classroom and the school. Perhaps as a result of this, teachers are often classified either as those who know their subjects and are "hard-nosed" or "no-nonsense" types, or as those who care for students, are warm-hearted but soft, and seem to have little command of their subjects. Those who are preparing to teach are too often torn between their sense of responsibility for content and their deep feeling for young people. These prospective teachers often choose to be one or the other type because they do not know how to be both a warm-hearted teacher who is skillful in interpersonal relations and also one who teaches important content effectively.

This series of books seeks to help teachers be both. The subtitles of the five books are **Interpersonal Skills, Content Development Skills, Lesson Planning Skills, Teaching Delivery Skills** and **Learning Management Skills**. The material in this series is based upon extensive practical experience as well as upon research.

To me, the most impressive feature of this series is its consistent emphasis upon the necessity for the student to internalize something before it is really learned. Unless the concept, the skill, the value, the attitude, or the interest has become part of the student's own thinking, feeling, or acting, it is not learned. Unless the teacher enters emphatically into the life and world of the student, he has not really learned interpersonal skills. Unless he finds his subject a resource on which students can draw in achieving their purposes, in solving their problems, and in making their lives more meaningful and happier, the teacher has not really developed his content for teaching. And unless he can design and organize learning experiences and can foresee vividly how he is to stimulate and guide students in these activities, the teacher has not really learned lesson planning skills. In creating this consistent emphasis, the authors have written in direct personal form. They avoid pedagogy and didactic exposition. This helps the reader to get a sense of working with children rather than observing them from afar.

Teachers and prospective teachers should find this series worth reading now for daily applications in the classroom. The **Skills of Teaching** series is also deserving of a place for continuing reference by all personnel concerned with the pursuit of excellence in education.

Ralph W. Tyler

Director Emeritus,
Center for Advanced Study
in the Behavioral Sciences,

Stanford, California

June, 1978

Getting a Job 1

Teaching Means Becoming a Learner Again

One of the biggest moments in your life comes the day you are assigned your first class to teach. It is an exciting time. A time of mixed emotions. You feel elated one minute and scared to death the next. It is a time for you to put to use all that you have learned. It is time for you to become a learner again. As much as you think you know about teaching, there is always more to learn.

Whether you are a beginning teacher or an experienced one, you take the job of teaching children seriously. You selected teaching as a profession because you wanted to help children grow. And because you take that job seriously, you know that you do not have all the answers.

Maria Burbank does not have all the answers either. She has completed her student teaching and is finishing up the last semester of her senior year at a state college. Experiencing Maria's transformation from student to teacher can help you gain insight into your own teaching experience. Compare your experiences with those of Maria. You will want to do all you can to improve your teaching delivery.

1

SIGNING THE CONTRACT

Maria dashed out of the Placement Office and collided with Lynn, who had been waiting for her in the corridor.

"I've got it! I've got it, Lynn!" Maria shouted at Lynn. In her excitement she grasped Lynn's shoulders and shook her.

"Hey! That's exciting, ole buddy," said Lynn. "Which one did you get? Tell me all about it."

"C'mon. Let's get outside. Oh! I'm just so excited I'm going to burst!" Maria pulled Lynn down the hallway of the administration building and out into the bright spring sunshine.

Settling down on the grass in the shade of a spreading tree, Maria recounted her talk with the dean of placement.

"Not that I have the job yet, Lynn," said Maria, more to caution herself than Lynn. "One of the schools where I did my practice teaching has asked me to apply for an opening they have. Dr. Joyce said that it's a really strong indication that they would hire me."

"How great for you, Maria." Lynn was sincerely happy for her friend. "What with jobs so scarce and all, you must feel lucky. Is it that neat school in the suburbs?" asked Lynn. "The one that you liked so much?"

Maria glanced down for a moment then shrugged her shoulders. Looking up again she said to Lynn cautiously, "Well, no. It's the other school." The restraint in her voice did not go unnoticed by Lynn.

"Oh! Then it must be the city school." Lynn looked at Maria with a twinkle in her eye. "You always did like the challenges, ole buddy!"

Maria smiled and drew an application form from a long white envelope. "I know it won't be the easiest job," she said. "But it is a job teaching kids, and that's what I want to do!"

"If I know you, Maria, you'll do a super job for those kids," added Lynn.

Later that week, Maria had her interview with several administrators and the principal of Washington School. Maria was just nervous enough to make herself pay attention. She wanted her interviewers to know that she cared about children. She wanted them to know that she would try hard to reach every child in her classroom. And she came across very well: as a young person who cared, as a young person who knew some things but not all things.

Maria left the interview knowing the job was hers if she wanted it. "I'd never know how good I really am if I took an easy job," she reasoned to herself. "I'll have to work pretty hard to reach all the kids in my class at Washington. But I was able to do it for six weeks of student teaching. I certainly should be able to make a difference if I have those kids for a whole year!"

Maria signed her contract with the city. Several weeks later, Lynn was offered a contract in a nearby suburb. Then the whirlwind of exams and commencement caught all the seniors up in a final excitement. And before the girls had time to think, they were standing in their caps and gowns listening to the Commencement speaker. And there it was. A time to move on. A time to grow.

LEARNING ABOUT THE LEARNERS

The summer stretched ahead of Maria. September seemed very far away. Yet she felt a sense of apprehension about her new job.

"I want to make sure I'm doing all I can to get ready for next year," she said aloud.

First, she planned to observe the class she would have next September before school let out this June. This year's teacher would be able to give her some information, too. Then she might spend some time going over the students' permanent records. And, of course, she wanted all the text-books and curriculum materials she would be teaching with.

"There certainly is a lot of information to process. I've got to have a way of remembering it all," she continued aloud. "I wonder. . ." Maria's voice trailed off. "A journal! That's it! I'll keep a journal of my first year of teaching. That way I'll be able to keep track of all that happens to me." Maria smiled as she thought, "Why I might even write the Great American Novel for teachers!"

Your Journal Will Help You Improve Your Teaching

Follow along with Maria's first year of teaching. As you read selected excerpts from her journal, you will begin to understand the many facets of teaching delivery. If you are a student teacher, tutor, aid, or classroom teacher, you may want to keep a similar journal. You will then have a record of your own teaching delivery.

As you study your own journal, you will discover what teaching skills you have already mastered. In other cases, you will see how you can apply your existing skills in different areas of your teaching. Finally, you will note the skills that you need to learn in order to make your teaching delivery as good as it can be.

I sure felt nervous today - going into Washington school to find out about my class for next year. The principal, Mr. Abbott, spoke with me first. Although he was surprised by my early visit, he was helpful. First he talked generally about the kind of children he has in his school.

"Let's face it, Miss Burbank. We are an inner-city school. Some of our problems have been caused by society. Others are of our own making. About one-third of your class will be on welfare. Many of your children will come from one-parent homes. The children at Washington School move within this city or between other cities frequently. It isn't what you would call a stable population."

He then set up an observation period for me with Mrs. Snow's class. She teaches most of the children I will have next year. Every eye was on me when Mrs. Snow introduced me to the class as their next year's teacher. And what looks! Some were friendly, others uninterested, and still others were mischievous looks. I took a seat in the back of the room while Mrs. Snow continued with her lesson. But most of her class was not with her. They looked around the room, at each other, or just about anywhere except at the source of learning. They were quiet enough so that Theresa, Tony and Patrice could interact with Mrs. Snow. These three students seemed to be the only "learners" in the classroom. The other children seemed merely to exist. At the end of the lesson, the class scurried around to get ready for gym class. Mrs. Snow offered to fill me in on the class during her free period.

"It's almost the end of the year. I don't know who's more anxious for it all to end. . . me or the kids. They're not bad kids. But what a mixture! Why, do you know, their reading levels go from the first grade to the ninth grade? Can you imagine trying to fill all those needs in one day? And the kids themselves. Did you see the small, nervous boy in the back row? John? Well, he has just come into the school. This is his third foster home placement since January. His mother abandoned five kids. He's the oldest. And Angela in the front row. . . the one with all the bracelets. She's a ward of the state, too. Next to Angela is Kenneth. Now, he's one you'll have to keep your eye on. He can think up more ways to get out of work. . . Listen to me run on! You'll be able to find this all out for yourself in September. Besides, I'm giving you the wrong impression. They really are good kids."

Honestly, I did feel down after talking with Mrs. Snow. I mean, she said she really liked the kids, but she couldn't wait to get rid of them. I finally decided that she was probably tired and needed a vacation. And when I thought about how I would teach that class, I just knew it would be different.

Next, Mr. Abbott had made an appointment for me with the guidance counselor. Miss Morse was not much older than myself. From her greeting, I knew we would get along well.

"Call me Lois. You've been to Elsie's class already? She runs a tight ship, doesn't she? You probably didn't get a chance to really study the kids. Here are their permanent records, which have the family background on each child and his or her I.Q. and Achievement test scores. Since many of these kids have trouble with verbal communication, I wouldn't make my judgments on their scores alone. Did you

notice John and Kenneth in Elsie's class. They both see the school psychologist twice a week. You know John's mother abandoned him? Kenneth's father is an alcoholic. He knocks Kenneth around when he's in his cups. We're keeping a close watch on the situation. Janet, the girl with the glasses and all the pigtails has a serious visual problem. She's blind in one eye and cannot see very well with the other. You can look over the records now, but your real information will come when you start teaching these kids in September. And re-member, I'm here to help you and the children whenever I can."

After leaving Lois' office, I felt much better. Here was another person who wanted to help the children. That meant she would be able to help me, too. We both had the same goals.

On my way out of the building, I stopped by the office to say goodbye to Mr. Abbott. His secretary told me with a smile that he was busy. . .playing ball with a group of older children during their recess. She handed me a packet of materials tied up neatly in an oak tag accordian pouch. While I was visiting Mrs. Snow and Lois Morse, he had put together all my textbooks, course outlines, and even a planning book that I would use next year. A note was slipped under the string that really made me feel good. It said:

Welcome to the team, Maria!

We sure can use you!

B. Abbott

So much happened to me today that my head is spinning. That's why I'm going to jot down the facts that I know about the children who will be my students.

Student Facts:

Family Background: Varied socio-economic levels

One-third on welfare

Many children from one-parent homes

Two foster home placements

Mobile population

Intellectual Background: Varied reading levels (1-9)

Special Needs: Two students visit psychologist twice a week

One student with serious vision problem

Finding Out About Your Learners

Using Maria's list as an example, write down information that you can find out about your learners before teaching them. Use the spaces below to categorize this information into the three categories that Maria used.

If you are writing a journal, include how you got the information and from whom. Try to stick to facts about your learners rather than hearsay.

FAMILY BACKGROUND: _____

_____

_____

_____

_____

INTELLECTUAL BACKGROUND: _____

_____

_____

_____

SPECIAL NEEDS: _____

_____

_____

_____

Maria's visit to Washington School had worked to her advantage. She had made a good impression on her new principal, Mr. Abbott. The other members of the faculty would hear about her conscientiousness from Mrs. Snow and Lois Morse. And she felt much more confident about her first job. Her imagination would not have to work overtime during the summer conjuring up imagined difficulties with the principal and the students. She had learned that she could trust her principal. The guidance counselor would help her with the students' problems. But more importantly, Maria had learned something about her learners. She had observed their lack of interest in learning. That was one of her major concerns. Having her content available to study over the summer would help her with that first hurdle. She would be able to match up those disinterested learners with an appropriate content. She would find a way to turn those children on to learning. Somehow, September no longer seemed so far away. Instead Maria thought, "I've got a lot to do to get ready. I had better get busy!"

Using Maria's Experience

How many of you plan to visit your new teaching assignment prior to the first day? Probably only an unusual few. No one will ask you to, or even suggest that it is a good idea. And yet, looking ahead, you can see the advantages to taking this initiative. Yes! You care about making a good impression. But no one has ever told you how. Of course, you want to learn all you can about your learners before your first day of teaching. You never thought of observing them a week or two before your assignment. You will feel more comfortable with your content if you have gotten your textbooks or course outlines before the school year begins. You will have to take responsibility for obtaining these materials since no one will offer to give them to you in advance.

If you are already teaching, then you can learn about next year's learners. Each year there will be new learners and new contents for you to teach. It is not too late to learn about these learners and their content needs before next year when they enter your classroom.

Preparing the Content 2

ORGANIZING THE YEARLY CONTENT

The heavily overcast sky threatened to empty its contents at any moment on the parched summer soil. As the first few drops splattered on the window pane of Maria's apartment, she turned away with a sigh. "Well, there goes my day of rest and recovery at the pool. Blast! Why does it always have to rain on my day off!" As she glanced around the room, her eyes rested on the oak tag pouch Mr. Abbott had given her several weeks ago. She felt a twinge of guilt. When Maria had left Washington School after her visit, she had been so eager to start getting her content ready. But then, her summer job and her new apartment, as well as some time with friends, left her without a minute to even think about September.

"Today's the day," she resolved. And immediately, Maria felt better. Picking up the pouch, she spilled its contents onto the couch. The bright colors and shiney covers of the textbooks brightened up the room. She took a group of stapled mimeographed pages headed: "To all Level 5 Language Arts Teachers." Curling up in a corner of the couch, she said to herself, "This is as good a place to start as any!"

As Maria skimmed the directive from the language arts coordinator, she noted the major goals of the program. "It seems as if the emphasis of the program is on reading and writing. Yes! Those seem to be the units that I'd teach for the year." Maria stopped. "Units! Now, that sounds familiar. Sure enough! That's from Ed. 201, Dr. Slater's class. What did he say . . .?"

11 **Examining Content Development**[1]

To develop your yearly content, you will need to organize what you will teach into at least five levels. There is no magic to the number five. That number just ensures a level of detail that is needed for effective teaching. To develop the five levels of your content, you will start to organize the content beginning with the name of **the course** or subject. Then you will list **the units** you plan to teach during the year. From each unit you will organize **the topics** or sections that the unit should include for your course. Under each topic you will write **the tasks** that the sections need. Finally, you will write **the daily skills** needed to complete these tasks.

The chart below illustrates this organization of the year's content. To develop the content, work from left to right. To deliver it, you will move in the opposite direction, starting with the skills.

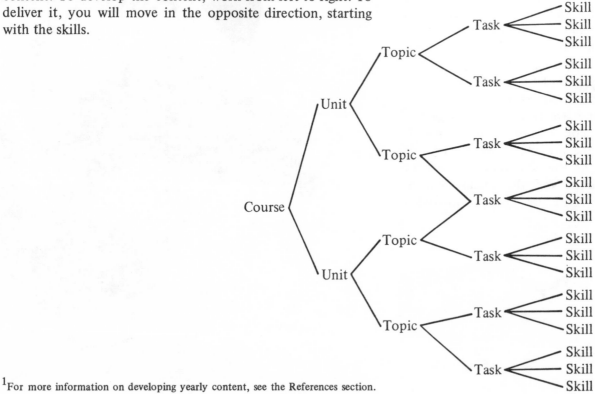

[1]For more information on developing yearly content, see the References section.

Naming the Course

One of the first steps to take when developing your content is to identify the course or subject that would include this area of study. You may be developing your content for fifth-grade mathematics, or eighth-grade social studies. You may be using a specific textbook as a guideline for your subject, or developing your content from scratch. In either case, the subject or **course** is the title of the content outline you will develop.

If you identify the title of your content, then the learners will know where the goal line is.

Defining the Units

After determining what the course is, you are ready to define the units you will teach over the year in that course. Units are the large divisions of the course. There should be at least two units to a course. Probably your course will have more than two. For example, you may want to divide your language arts content into four units: spelling, grammar, writing paragraphs, and reading. But there are no set rules which say that this is the only way to organize language arts. That is because the learners in different situations have their special needs. Another teacher may select three units for the learners: reading, writing, and speaking. Each set of units is as potentially effective as the other. That is because each unit will be divided into three more levels. And when each content is complete in respect to the learners, these units could very well contain identical elements, but appearing in a different sequence.

Another way to determine the units of your content, is to look at the table of contents in your course's textbooks. Where several chapters are grouped under one heading, you have the name of a unit. You may have to examine several textbooks before you find this level of detail in the table of contents.

If you break the course into units, then the learners will be able to organize what they learn.

Listing the Topics of the Content

The third level of content organization involves listing the topics into which you want to divide the units. Each unit should have at least two topics. But again, there is no set number of topics for any unit. Nor do the number of topics have to be the same under the units. One unit may have two topics; another may have nine. These numbers will depend upon how you choose to organize your content. Look once again at your textbook's table of contents. The topics of a unit are really its chapters. For example, in a grammar text the chapters may be: capitalization, punctuation, verbs, and nouns. These will become the topics of the unit. When you write your content, use action verbs to describe what you want the learners to be able to do: **use, solve, analyze, read, write,** and **compare** are examples of words that describe what you want the learners to be able to do when they complete the topic or the unit.

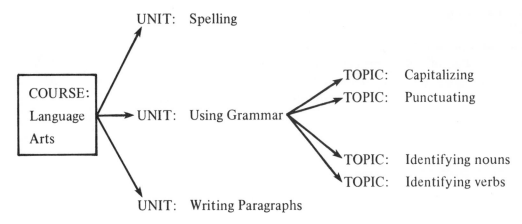

Finding the Tasks

The fourth step in organizing your yearly content involves finding tasks for each topic. This requires a careful scrutiny of each topic's elements in relation to the unit and the course. Each level is dependent on the one above to make a coherent content. There will be at least two tasks under each topic. It would be advisable to refer again to several textbooks' tables of contents. Under each chapter or topic, you will probably find a list of tasks for that topic. In a language arts course, you may find the following tasks: reviewing action verbs, reviewing auxiliary verbs, determining tenses, and understanding non-standard forms. A word of caution at this point, however: remember that the tasks still have to be broken into at least two daily skills. Therefore, you will want to consider a task as part of your content when a task takes two days to a week to teach.

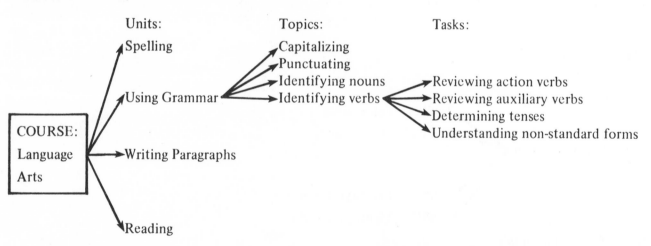

Examining The Skills of The Content

The final step of organizing your content is to determine what the daily skills under each task are. Let's stop to take a closer look at what we mean by "skills." **Skills are what you want your learners to be able to do**. They are things that the learners will learn how to do while they are studying the tasks you have developed. Skills are **measurable**. You can determine how well your learners perform them. Skills are **repeatable**. Your learners have a way to perform the skill again and again. Skills are **observable**. You can watch your learners perform them. Using these three criteria, the following skills could be included under the "action verb" task of the example given earlier: supplying the missing verb, changing the form of the verb, and identifying the verb in a simple sentence. To determine what daily skills make up each task, you will have to leave a textbook's table of contents and go directly to its inner pages.

If you teach skills, your learners will be able to act with the new learning.

"Five levels of yearly content, huh?" Maria looked down at the empty pages in front of her. "My only problem is that my learners are at so many different levels that I'll have to write more than one yearly content." She furrowed her brow with a scowl. "This directive from the coordinator is okay for the students in my class who are reading within a year of grade level. Let's see . . . how many kids would that be?" Maria drew out her class list to which she added the individual reading levels of each student. She counted up eight chil-

dren who were reading within a year of their grade level. There were three students who were reading more than two years above grade level. Seven students were one to two years behind, and five students were more than two years below grade level.

"For now, I'll work on the grade level students' content." And using her texts and the other resource materials included in the packet from Mr. Abbott, she outlined the first unit for these "average" readers in her journal.

COURSE   **UNITS**   **TOPICS**   **TASKS**   **SKILLS**

Language Arts

- Spelling
- Using Grammar
  - Capitalizing
  - Punctuating
  - Identifying nouns
  - Identifying verbs
    - Reviewing action verbs
    - Reviewing auxiliary verbs
    - Determining tenses
    - Understanding non-standard forms
      - Supplying the missing verbs
      - Changing the form of the verbs
      - Identifying the verb in a simple sentence
- Writing Paragraphs
- Reading

Language Arts - Group C

I. Reading

A. Reading the Short Story

1. Describing the Story

a. Describing the setting orally
b. Illustrating the setting
c. Describing the problem orally
d. Answering objective questions about the problem
e. Describing the main events orally
f. Sequencing the main events orally

2. Describing the Characters

a. Describing their appearance orally
b. Illustrating their appearance
c. Describing their relationship to the plot orally
d. Answering objective questions about them
e. Analyzing their roles orally
f. Comparing them with other characters from other reading orally

B. Giving a Book Report

1. Giving an Oral Book Report

a. Using correct posture and voice
b. Speaking in complete sentences
c. Preparing an opening sentence
d. Describing the main points
e. Preparing an ending sentence

2. Writing a Report

a. Writing an opening sentence
b. Writing a sentence that describes the setting
c. Writing a description of the major characters
d. Writing a description of the plot
e. Writing a closing sentence

Outlining Your Yearly Content

You should be able to outline at least one unit of a yearly content you expect to teach. Select a content that you know well. You will carry this content throughout this book. First you will develop the content, then plan several lessons, and finally practice delivering that content. If you are keeping a journal of your teaching experience, include this content in that journal.

COURSE: _____

I. UNIT: _____

   A. TOPIC: _____

      1. TASK: _____

         a. SKILL: _____

_____

_____

_____

_____

_____

_____

_____

Maria was startled by a loud knock at the door. "It's me, Maria! Lynn!"

Hurrying to open the door for her friend, Maria said, "Come in! Come in!"

Lynn shook out her dripping raincoat and followed Maria over to the couch. They talked excitedly with one another about all that had happened since their last visit. Finally, Maria rose and said, "I'm starving. What about lunch?"

"Sounds great," answered Lynn. "How about one of your midnight specials?" She started to follow Maria into the kitchen. "Hey! What's all this?" she paused at the desk, taking the content outline in her hands. "Honestly, Maria, you're the limit. Here it's July and you're already planning for September."

"I've finally gotten to that stuff Mr. Abbott gave me," Maria called from the kitchen. "It is a lot of work. Especially since I've got to have four reading groups at least!"

"You're crazy, Maria! FOUR contents in reading! FOUR groups of kids learning FOUR different daily skills. Why, that's just like the 'Bluebirds' and the 'Robins'. You can't do that!"

"Why not, for heaven's sake," responded Maria from her sandwich-making. "Those kids aren't going to learn any other way."

Lynn stood in the doorway, keeping out of Maria's way. "But the kids will know that they're in the dummy group! You'll end up giving them a complex or something," continued Lynn.

"You think if I try to teach them all the same thing they won't know that they are slow learners," responded Maria. "Be realistic, Lynn! They know that they can't read as well as the other kids. And the other kids know it, too." Maria turned back to her sandwich-making. "Why, they would be so out of it they wouldn't learn a thing. But what's more important is that they would know I was trying to fool them

about how good they are. They'd never trust me again!"

Holding up her hands as if giving up, Lynn said, "Okay! Okay! Don't get so upset! I just thought the 'Bluebirds' were out."

"Maybe the 'Bluebirds' are out but teaching is in. And if I'm any kind of a teacher, I will teach those kids what they are ready to learn."

Using Maria's Experience

How many of you will consider how well your students match up with the content you have selected to teach? Answering the question of grouping is one of the primary steps toward developing your completed content. You may decide that the skills of your yearly content are inappropriate for some of your students to learn. If so, you will then have to write another more appropriate content to match the abilities and achievement of these students. It goes without saying that if you have heterogeneous grouping you should have more than one yearly content. This may also be true for some homogeneous groups. In either case, it will mean more work for you to teach more than one content to your class. But the added work will pay off in the success your learners will have in acquiring new skills.

"I suppose I'll have to have groups for some of the classes I'm going to teach," said Lynn finishing up her salami, bologna, pickle and hot pepper sandwich. "Oh, Maria! You keep me honest! Hey, listen. I've got to be at work in an hour but what about leaving the city next weekend? My parents are at the shore. We could surprise them."

"Sounds great, Lynn. I'd love to," said Maria helping Lynn into her damp raincoat.

After Lynn had left, Maria went back to her desk and began developing the details of the yearly content she had developed in the morning. "I could go ahead and develop the yearly content for the other three groups," she thought. "But it would probably be best to stay on one content at a time."

"If I remember correctly, there were five levels to the daily content, too. Now, what was it Dr. Slater said? Facts. Concepts. Yes! That's it."

Considering The Daily Content[2]

    In developing your **daily skills** content, you will begin by developing **the skill steps** that your learners will follow to perform the skill. Once you have developed the skill steps, you will want to identify the supportive knowledge that your learners will need to know in order to perform the skill steps. The first level of supportive knowledge is **the facts**. Facts are the names or labels we attach to things to make an identification. **The concepts** are the second level of supportive knowledge. Concepts are the meanings or notions we attach to things. The third level of supportive knowledge is **the principles**. Principles usually show a cause-and-effect relationship concerning some aspect of the skill. They can usually be stated using the "if . . . then . . ." format. The following chart shows the combination of the yearly content with the daily content.

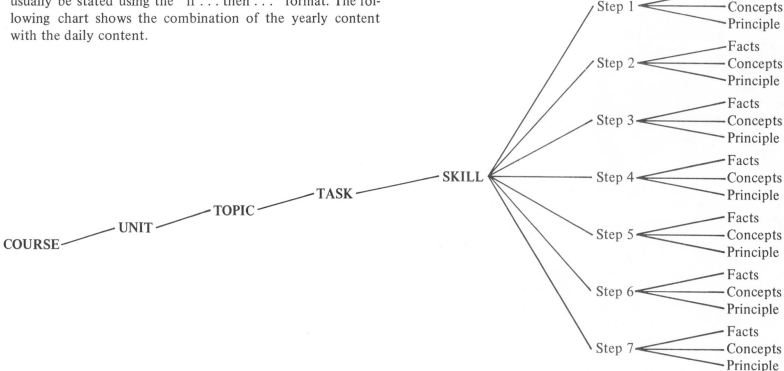

[2]For more information on developing daily content, see the References section.

Taking Another Look at Skills

Before you begin to learn how to write skill steps, you should be sure that you have a skills content. Remember, to be a skill, the learners have to **do** something. Writing a list of words or phrases from memory, or labeling a diagram are not skills in the true sense of the word. There are skills involved: the skill of recall, and the skill of copying. But these are not the kinds of skills that you want the learners to focus on. You want them to learn skills like outlining, multiplication, research, and scientific investigation. These are skills with which you can observe and measure your learners' performance. The students should also be able to repeat these skills. When you develop skill steps, ask: "Is this what I want my learners to learn to do?"

If your content contains skills, then you will help your learners to be more successful in learning.

Identifying The Skill

To begin writing the **skill** steps of the daily content, you need a statement of the end result. That is, what your learners will be able to **do** when they complete the **skill** steps. This statement describes the skill objective that you want your learners to achieve. For example, you may want the learners to supply the missing verbs in a sentence. Then the skill statement is: Supply the missing verb in a sentence.

COURSE

1. Unit

  A. Topic

    1. Task

      a. Skill

Identifying The First Skill Step

You must now determine what is the very first thing your learners must do to attain this skill. If you want the learners to supply the missing verb in a sentence, their first step would be to read the sentence. It is critical that your learners succeed in doing the first step, if they are ever to reach the last. If the learners can complete the first step successfully, they will be able to attempt the next step in your daily program.

COURSE

1. Unit

   A. Topic

      1. Task

         a. Skill

           1) Step

Once you have written the first **skill** step, you can continue to write the remaining skill steps. These steps will bring your learners from the first step to the last. They will culminate in the learners' being able to perform the skill. For example, after reading a sentence missing a verb, ask yourself: "What do the learners have to do in order to fill in the correct missing verb?" Thinking through what you would do, you may write the following steps: 1) read the sentence; 2) place the first verb on your list in the blank and reread the sentence; 3) ask yourself if the sentence makes sense; 4) insert the next word into the sentence; 5) ask yourself if the sentence makes sense with that word in it; 6) continue testing all the listed words. It is important to include all the steps that your learners need to take in order to complete the skill. A reaction like, "I did what you said but it still doesn't come out right," means that you have failed to personalize the development of steps in terms of the learners' frames of reference. Test the skill steps by doing the skill yourself, following the steps you have written.

COURSE

1. UNIT

    A. Topic

        1. Task

            a. Skill

                1) Step

                2) Step

                3) Step

                4) Step

                5) Step

Writing the Remaining Skill Steps

As you write the remaining steps of your daily content, you will ask yourself if they adequately describe what your learners must do in order to complete the skill. Many learners fail because they cannot supply the steps that are missing: "I thought I had it, but I goofed!" The only reason that some succeed, is that they are able to supply these steps: "Oh boy, it really works!"

You can expedite the learning process when you teach your learners all the steps they need to learn. These steps should be small enough for the learners to follow them easily. Remember to check to see if you can perform the skill successfully by following the steps you have written.

Developing the Supportive Knowledge

You have taken your content and broken it down into more detail starting with the course that you teach. As you develop the content, you move from the units through successive levels. Once you develop the skills level of the content, you are focusing on the daily content to be taught. Your learners should learn the principle of what the skill does: "How come this works like this?" They will need to learn certain facts and concepts that are included in the skill steps: "What's this part called? What's it do?" We group together facts, concepts, and principles as the supportive knowledge of the skill.

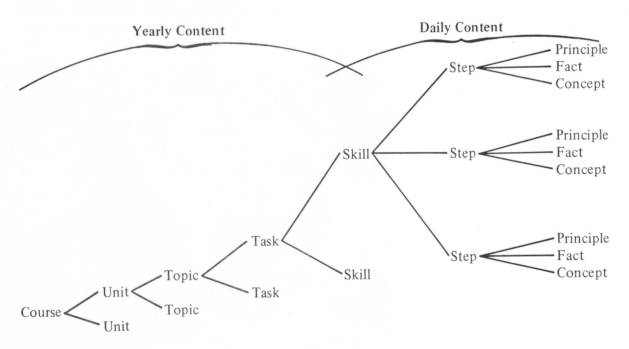

Identifying The Facts

The first thing that you want to do is to identify the facts related to the skills you are teaching. The facts are the simplest things to learn about the skill. Facts are the names or labels we attach to things to identify them. They are nouns that answer the question, "What is it?" In relation to a skill, facts are the things involved in performing its steps. Most often, facts are the names of people, places, and things. As you may already know, teaching facts by themselves is dangerous because there is so little you can do with them. We communicate about things by just using their names. They are particularly important to know for tests. But in the final analysis, you cannot **implement** facts. Thus, facts are considered a primary support level of knowledge because they enable learners to talk about what they are learning to do.

Your learners need to know facts so that you can tell and show them about the new learning.

Identifying The Concepts

What you know **about** a fact is called a **concept**. Concepts describe the nature or characteristics of things. Therefore, adjectives and adverbs are concepts. Concepts describe what something does. Thus, verbs are also concepts. Concepts are what we know about something. This is why our levels of knowledge involve all we know about something — even how to implement it. Your concept of "sitting" enables you to recognize the object you sit on as a chair, even if it doesn't have legs. A child's concept of "hot" may be identical to the object, or fact — "stove." Later, the child will attach additional facts and concepts to the word "hot" such as "match," "friction," and "molecular motion," as his or her knowledge of "hotness" expands.

"I know another way to get something hot! Make it go around and rub against something else — like the tires on my Mom's car!"

"Great Sheila! It's really fun to discover new ways of doing something, isn't it?"

Your learners need to know concepts so that they can understand how to perform the skill steps.

Concepts are the Second Level of Knowledge

What can your learners do with concepts? If facts are the names of things, then your learners may, at some point, only know one fact about something. Conceptual learning enables the learners to organize what they know. They can name what they know and can tell you one or more things about what they know. But in the final analysis, they cannot **implement** a concept any more than they can implement a fact. Concepts can only be recalled.

"What is that?"

"A butterfly (fact)."

"Why?"

"Because it has large (concept), colored (concept) wings (fact)."

"Because it is pretty (concept)."

"Right (concept). And I bet you feel pretty smart because you knew all those answers!"

COURSE

1. UNIT

  A. Topic

    1. Task

      a. Skill

        1) Step

          a) Facts

          b) Concepts

Identifying The Principles

There are many principles related to every skill you teach. One kind of principle describes **why** or **how** something works the way it does. This principle helps the learner to understand how his or her world works. It's the answer to the four-year-old's "Why?" "When the big hand goes around one time, one hour has passed." "If you use a ruler to steady the pencil, the line will be straighter." "If you increase the angle of an inclined plane, then the effort needed to push the block will also increase." Each of these principles deals with the idea of "cause and effect." They explain a cause-and-effect relationship for some aspect of the skill. Note that the principle deals only with the content and not with its relationship to the learner.

"So if I write a good topic sentence for my paragraph, then I'll be identifying the main idea of the paragraph, so that I can make every other sentence relate to that one!"

"Yes, Nancy, and you will feel more sure of yourself when you have a way to check your topic sentences!"

If _____ , then _____ .

The format of this content principle will help you recognize it when you see one. A principle can usually be phrased in an "If   , then   " statement. Following the "if" is the cause. Following the "then" is the effect. "If you face your teacher squarely and lean toward her, then you are paying attention." Cause and effect. "If you outline your paper before writing it, your ideas will build upon each other." The "if" is the skill you are teaching your learners, while the "then" is the benefit from the skill itself. Your learners can now understand how the skill works.

Principles are the Third Level of Knowledge

It will be sufficient for you to write one principle for each daily skill content. That principle should link the skill to the learner. You will write the principle of the skill leading to the function of the skill. If you describe the setting of a short story, then you will know when and where that story took place. Examining this last principle, you will note that the "cause" is really the skill. The "effect" is what happens when the learner performs the skill. Very simply, then, you can write a principle for your daily content using the format: If (**skill**) then (**function of the skill**).

COURSE

1. UNIT

  A. Topic

    1. Task

      a. Skill (Principle)

        1) Step

          a) Facts

          b) Concepts

        2) Step

          a) Facts

          b) Concepts

        3) Step

          a) Facts

          b) Concepts

"I've got to remember that the skill steps are what the learners are supposed to do," said Maria to herself. "That's where I had a lot of trouble in Dr. Slater's course. I kept writing what I was going to do to teach the skill or what the learners had to do to learn the skill. But once I understood that the skill steps are what the learners do to perform the skill, it was okay! My learners were able to follow the steps to complete the skill successfully. Let's try it with my first daily skill."

Maria wrote the following skill steps in her journal. Then she added the important words (facts and concepts) that her learners would have to learn in order to perform the steps. Under the skill, she included the principle of what the skill does.

Skill: Describing the Setting of a Short Story Orally

    Principle: (If you describe the setting of a short story, then
                 you will know when and where the story takes place.)

    Step 1:   Read the Short Story

        Fact: Short Story

    Step 2:   Answer the Question: Where does the story take place?

        Concept: Where

        Facts: Country, Urban, Suburban, Rural, Wilderness

    Step 3:   Answer the Question: When does the story take place?

        Concept: When

        Facts: Past, Present, Future

    Step 4:   Say, The story takes place__(when)__ in __(where)__ .

"It should be enough to develop the daily content for just my first units of the yearly content," thought Maria to herself. "Once I start teaching, I may have to change this content. Some of my learners may need more skills to complete the task. Perhaps some of them can skip some of these skills that I'm including. That's even true of the skill steps. Here again, some learners will need more skill steps to complete the skill, while others will need less."

Maria wrinkled up her nose as she thought about all the work that lay ahead. "Well, kid! You asked for it! No one ever told you that teaching was a soft job! And now you're beginning to realize just how much work it is."

Outlining Your Daily Content

Using the first daily skill of the yearly content you out-lined, write the skill steps and the supportive knowledge for that skill. You may wish to consult other resource materials to help you write the skill steps. Remember that the steps are what the learners **do**, not what they should know. Since practice makes perfect, you could practice writing the daily content for your first unit of the yearly content. This com-pleted unit should be included in your journal.

SKILL: _____

   PRINCIPLE: _____

     SKILL STEP 1: _____

       CONCEPTS: _____

       FACTS: _____

     SKILL STEP 2: _____

       CONCEPTS: _____

       FACTS: _____

     SKILL STEP 3: _____

       CONCEPTS: _____

       FACTS: _____

39

SKILL STEP 4: _____

CONCEPTS: _____

FACTS: _____

SKILL STEP 5: _____

CONCEPTS: _____

FACTS: _____

_____

_____

_____

Using Maria's Experience

Before you begin teaching, will you prepare several weeks of daily content? Many of you will answer, "No!" You may not receive any materials ahead of time. You may wait until you meet with your supervisors. For others, you may want to see your students before you make any plans. There are just so many different things to do, you are not sure where to start.

When you develop several weeks of your daily content, you are more prepared to meet your learners for the first time. You can direct your full attention to those learners. Using that developed content as a yardstick, you can see how your learners measure up to that content. Your preparation frees you to focus on your learners.

WRITING A LESSON PLAN

Maria reached into her mailbox and took out several letters and a large manila envelope. Keeping one foot in the vestibule door to hold it open, she juggled her pocketbook, keys, and mail to get a better look at the ochre envelope. There it was . . . the letter she had been waiting for all summer. Entering the lobby of her apartment building, she automatically pushed the elevator button, tearing open the envelope as she waited. The cover memo was addressed: TO WASHINGTON SCHOOL STAFF MEMBERS.

"It's about time," thought Maria. "I've had enough of summer!" It had been a good summer for Maria and a busy one. But sne was ready to leave her summer's cleric's job and sink her teeth into teaching.

Letting herself into her apartment, she went into the kitchen. She filled a glass with iced tea and settled down at the table to review the contents of the envelope. There in front of her was the first of a collection of forms, memos, and lists. A collection that would grow in alarming proportions over the next ten months. There was a notice of orientation for new teachers, a schedule for all teachers to follow on their work day, class lists, and advisories from curriculum supervisors.

"Well! It looks as if the administration is ready for the teachers. Maybe I had better get ready for my students!"

That night, after she had eaten, Maria got out her oak tag pouch of materials and the content she had outlined in July. "I want to write out my lesson plans for the first week," she thought. "I know that my students will make up their minds about me on that first day. It will be important for me to start off on the right foot."

Leaning back in her chair, she remembered first days of school she had known. "It was so exciting getting ready for that first day. Every year was going to be the year I really **did** something! But that first day . . . it was such an anticlimax. Instead of doing something, I had to listen to the teacher go on and on about the rules I had to follow in class!"

Maria shook her head. "It's not going to be like that my first day of teaching. My learners will be busy doing things the very first day!"

She took out some fresh paper. "I did enough of these lesson plans for Dr. Cullen, my supervisor, in student teaching. I should be able to do a good job on plans for my own class. As I remember there were five sections . . ."

Divide the content of that lesson into five sections: review, overview, presentation, exercise, and summary. The acronym, ROPES, will help you remember this organization.

One of the first things you should plan is what to review before you teach the new skill. Ask yourself, **"What other skills do my learners need to be able to do before they can do the new skill?"** For example, to write a correct sentence, your learners need to be able to write, spell, and identify the subject and predicate. To multiply by a two-digit number, the learners need to have addition and regrouping skills. The beginning of the lesson is an appropriate time to review these **contingency skills** which your students have already learned. The skill you taught the previous day may be a contingency skill or closely related to the new skill. The learners may have learned the contingency skill last year. In any case, before you begin to teach the new skill, you should review any contingency skills.

LESSON PLANNING SKILLS

Content

Organization   Reviewing

Content   Contingency

            Skill Steps

[3]For more information on organizing the content of a lesson plan, see the References section.

Reviewing Facilitates Diagnosis

The review is a significant part of your lesson plan. You will use the review to diagnose where the learners are.

"Can they perform the contingency skills?"

"Do you need to teach a simpler skill or one that is more complex?"

After you teach your learners how to do the contingency skill, you will answer these questions when the learners perform the contingency skill. You will be able to observe the level of the skills that your learners have.

When you review, you can diagnose your learners.

Overviewing Applications

When you **overview** the new skill with your learners, you are, in effect, **giving them a reason for learning the new skill**. You know what your reason is for teaching the new skill. It is one link in the chain of skills that make up your curriculum. Your students need to learn how to multiply before they learn how to divide. Unless they iearn to multiply, they will have to write long, long columns of addition. Multiplication is much faster than addition. You have a perspective on the problem that your learners do not have. You will try to share that perspective in the overview.

LESSON PLANNING SKILLS

Content Organization	Reviewing		Overviewing
			▽
Content	Contingency Skill Steps		Skill Applications

Teaching Skill Applications

Your overview really involves teaching the applications or uses of the skill to the learners. It reminds the learners that what they are learning today is just a small piece of tomorrow's larger picture. In addition, the overview helps them to diagnose themselves in relation to that picture. When it comes down to the wire, you may find that the learners are very concerned about their lack of printing ability. You may hear them say:

"Mine always looks so messy! Uck!"

"I'm just a slob, I guess!"

"You think I'll be able to do it right, huh?"

Where the review helps the teacher diagnose the learners' readiness to learn the new skill, the overview helps the learners diagnose their own readiness to learn that skill. Once the teacher and the learners are aware of where the learners stand, they are ready for the presentation of the new skill.

When you overview the new skill, your learners can diagnose themselves in relation to the new skill.

Presenting Skill Steps

After you have written the content for the review and overview of the skill you plan to teach, you are ready to attack the **presentation**. You will teach your learners **how to perform the skill**. To do this, you need to break that skill down into the steps your learners take to perform the skill. This is critical to the success of your planning and delivery as far as your learners are concerned. As simple as it sounds, it takes practice to be able to break down the skills you teach into the learner-size steps. How many times have you heard your learners say:

"What do I do first?"

"We don't know where to begin!"

"What do we do next?"

What your learners are really asking you for are the steps they need to perform the skill successfully.

LESSON PLANNING SKILLS

Content Organization	Reviewing	→	Overviewing	→	Presenting
Content	Contingency Skill Steps		Skill Applications		Skill Steps

Exercising Skill Steps

The next part of your lesson plan organization is the **exercise**. The learners need the opportunity to perform the new skill. The learners will have already been taught how to perform the steps of the skill in the **presentation**. They may have had an opportunity to do the skill at least once. But once is not enough. The **exercise** of the lesson does not introduce any new content but **involves the learners in repeated use of the new skill**. The skill will be performed by itself. Then the learners will do exercises which have them use the new skill in conjunction with other skills. The more times you can involve your learners in using the new skill, the more you increase their chances of being able to master the new skill. A variety of practice materials and applications will keep the learning exciting.

Content Organization	Reviewing	▶	Overviewing	▶	Presenting	▶	Exercising
	⇩		⇩		⇩		⇩
Content	Contingency Skill Steps		Skill Application		Skill Steps		Skill Steps

Teaching the Exercise

You have always known how important it is for the learners to practice the new learning. Practice does make perfect provided the **exercise** is meaningful. You understand that the learners should use the materials needed to perform the particular skill. You will select materials for the exercise that they will have success with. Then you will study the applications of the skill to determine what other skills the learners use when they practice the new skill. If the practice includes skills the learners have not learned, they will fail. So you will select the applications which use the new skill in conjunction with skills the learners have already mastered. Then you may hear your learners say:

"So that's how it works!"
"Now I can do it!"
"That's NEAT!"

When you have the learners exercise they have an opportunity to practice the skill.

Summarizing Skill Steps

The final part of your lesson is a **summary**. This gives you another opportunity to **review the new skill with your learners**. They may have forgotten a step or not fully understood a part of what they were doing in the exercise. You summarize the steps of performing the skill. Then you can diagnose where your learners are in relation to what you have taught. Your learners can use the summary to diagnose themselves in relation to what they have learned.

Content Organization	Reviewing	▶	Overviewing	▶	Presenting	▶	Exercising	▶	Summarizing
▽	▽		▽		▽		▽		▽
Content	Contingency Skill Steps		Skill Application		Skill Steps		Skill Steps		Skill Steps

When you summarize, the learners have an opportunity to review what they have learned.

You have just learned how to use ROPES to organize the content of the lesson. Take the time to read the summary below. You should be more confident in your use of ROPES to organize your content.

Review A short time is spent at the beginning of class reviewing any contingency skills which the learners may need in order to perform the new skill. (Content: Skill steps of the contingency skill)

Overview A few minutes are spent showing how the new skill works. In addition, the learners are taught the applications of where and when they can use the new skill. (Content: Principles and applications of the new skill).

Presentation Five to ten minutes are spent teaching the skill steps of the new skill to the learners. This includes any facts and concepts the learners do not understand. (Content: Skill steps of the new skill and facts and concepts of these steps)

Exercise The predominant part of your lesson is spent in having the learners practice the new skill. First they will repeat the new skill and then apply the new skill. (Content: Skill steps, facts, concepts, and principles)

Summary A brief part of the lesson is spent reviewing the new skill for the learners. (Content: Skill steps, facts, concepts, principles)

51

Looking back to the daily content of her first lesson, Maria jotted down the following notes. She wanted her daily content to fit ROPES. She wrote in her journal.

Skill: *Describing the Setting of a Short Story in a Complete Sentence*

Review: *Contingency Skill - Describing the Setting of an Illustration*

1. *Examine the illustration for detail.*
2. *Determine where the picture was taken.*
3. *Determine when the picture was taken.*
4. *Say: This picture was taken (where) in (when)*

Overview: *Principle - If you know when and where a story takes place, then you will be able to anticipate what could happen in the story.*

Presentation: *Skill Steps:*

1. *Read story.*
2. *Determine where story takes place:*
   Where - City, Suburb, Rural, Wilderness
3. *Determine when story takes place:*
   When - Past, Present, Future
4. *Write: The story takes place in (where) in (when)*

Exercise: *Skill steps, facts, concepts and principles as above.*

Summary: *Skill steps, facts, concepts and principles as above.*

PLANNING THE METHODS

"Good ole 'Tell-Show-Do' Cullen. I'm going to miss that funny lady!" Maria smiled to herself, thinking back to her Methods of Teaching professor. "Teachers like that don't come along that often. Sure, the other kids used to laugh at her with all her bags and boxes of gadgets. She had found so many different methods in her years of experience she just overwhelmed us. Why, she could think of more different ways to use a clothespin in the classroom than Heloise."

"Methods! That's what I have to plan now for my first lesson plan."

Telling Names, Definitions, Reasons, and Steps[4]

Next, you decide what methods to use with your ROPES content. Telling is the most common source of learning. From many teachers' frames of reference, the easiest way to deliver is to tell the learners what they need to know. In other words, they lecture. Telling is essential (but not sufficient) for your teaching delivery. You tell your learners about the new learning. If they need a fact such as the name of an object, you will tell them what it is called; for example, an "internal combustion engine." Your learners may need concepts which are the definitions of new terms. You tell them "compression is when the piston moves up in the cylinder, squeezing the fuel and air mixture." In a like manner, you **tell** your learners about the principles that explain why things work that way when you say "the exploding gases push the piston down." **Telling** your learners how to perform the steps of a skill could include **saying** that "the first step is to check the spark plugs to see if they need replacement."

LESSON PLANNING SKILLS

Content Organization	Reviewing	Overviewing	Presenting	Exercising	Summarizing
Content	Contingency Skill Steps	Skill Applications	Skill Steps	Skill Steps	Skill Steps
Methods	Telling	Telling	Telling	Telling	Telling

[4]For more information on planning the methods of a lesson plan, see the References section.

Telling Helps Your Auditory Learners

Examine the different kinds of learners you have in your class. The learners who are predominantly auditory listen to you intently. You tell them what to do and they do it. These learners will tend to interact in classroom discussions more than other kinds of learners. Because they are predominantly auditory, they will also learn well from written material. Your delivery will meet the needs of your auditory learners when you tell them about what they need to know.

Some learners learn best from **tell** methods like written materials.

Telling the Learners What You Want Them to Learn

Using **tell** methods is one of your teaching delivery skills. **Tell** methods answer the question:

"What am I going to use to **tell** my class what they want or need to learn?"

For the moment, you may take the safe side and select methods which simply **tell** the learners what they are to learn. For example, there are a variety of **tell** sources available to you: you, another teacher, a learner, or a guest speaker. In addition, there is a variety of equipment that can be employed by these sources to tell; an audiotape, a videotape, a record, textbook, worksheet, transparency, or a poster. All of these could be used as **tell** methods. While most **tell** methods are auditory, there are some that are visual. All **tell** methods deal with words, either spoken or written.

Telling methods let your learners hear what they should learn.

Showing Names, Definitions, Reasons, and Steps

Another method you must use in delivering content is to **show** the learners what they want or need to learn. **Showing** is a critical source of learning. When you tell your learners that it is called "an internal combustion engine," you should also **show** them what the engine looks like. When you explain a concept like the definition of compression, you should **show** your learners a diagram of the compression cycle. Before you tell your learners about the expansion of the hot gas, you may want to **show** your learners what happens to a balloon when the gas inside is heated. Your **show** method visually explains the principle your learners need in order to understand the power cycle of the engine. You will also **tell** and **show** the steps of performing the skill. Then, when you **tell** the learners to check the spark plug, you **show** them how at the same time.

LESSON PLANNING SKILLS

Content Organization	Reviewing	Overviewing	Presenting	Exercising	Summarizing
Content	Contingency Skill Steps	Skill Application	Skill Steps	Skill Steps	Skill Steps
Methods	Telling Showing	Telling Showing	Telling Showing	Telling Showing	Telling Showing

Showing Helps Your Visual Learners

Some of your learners are predominantly visual. They develop a mental picture from the descriptive words you use. When you show them a picture, these learners become very involved in the learning. They see details and draw conclusions that amaze you. Your visual learners will also like to make their own pictures of what they are learning. They may even be your "daydreamers" because of the mental pictures they can conjure up so easily. While **tell** methods deal with words, **show** methods deal with pictures. The proverb "one picture is worth a thousand words" was probably coined by a visual learner.

Showing methods let your learners see what they should learn.

Showing the Learners What You Want Them to Learn

A picture, a diagram, a series of pictures, or the action of performing the skill are what the **show** methods deliver to your learners. The most common **show** method is the demonstration. That is because the teacher does that **showing**. There are other options, however.

You may want to teach your learners how to splice an electric wire. You will, of course, **tell** them how to do it and you will also **show** them how to do it. You may ask a learner who already has the skill to demonstrate. You could use a film, slides, pictures, overhead or opaque projectors, a poster, a model, a mock-up, or an exhibit to teach the skill with a series of pictures. You may use any one or several of these as **show** methods.

Some learners need to be shown what to do.

Do Methods Help Learners Acquire Names, Definitions, Reasons, and Skills

Tell and **show** are methods that the teacher uses to communicate the new learning. **Do** methods are used to involve all learners in the performance of the new skill. These **do** methods are actually learning experiences the teacher plans so that the learners can participate. A laboratory which asks the learners to identify a mineral allows everyone to manipulate a mineral and the testing equipment. The learners actually perform the skill of identifying a mineral.

The teacher uses learning experiences when new words and definitions have to be learned, too. Planning activities which have the learners use these facts and concepts will involve them in writing, speaking, or drawing. Keeping a list of geology definitions or diagramming a volcano are **do** methods which have the learners use the new facts and concepts they need to learn. A field trip around the school grounds can have the learners discovering eroded soil, gullies, cracked rocks, or decaying plant material, which illustrate the principles of weathering and erosion. As a **do** method, you may choose to have your learners map and label the areas where these things are occurring.

LESSON PLANNING SKILLS

Content Organization	Reviewing	Overviewing	Presenting	Exercising	Summarizing
Content	Contingency Skill Steps	Skill Application	Skill Steps	Skill Steps	Skill Steps
Methods	Telling Showing Doing	Telling Showing Doing	Telling Showing Doing	Telling Showing Doing	Telling Showing Doing

Doing Helps Everyone Learn What Has Been Told and Shown

Some of your learners are kinesthetic learners. They learn by moving things, manipulating, and performing. These learners will sit back while you tell or show what is to be done . . . but not for long. After a while, they begin to fidget. As soon as they have an inkling of what the assignment is, they are ready to begin. It doesn't matter if you have not even finished giving the directions. They just want to "get busy."

"Let me do that!"

"It's my turn!"

The visual learners need to **see** how to perform the new skill. The auditory learners need to **hear** what they should do. But all of your learners need the opportunity to **do** the skill. The real learning for all of us takes place when we perform the skills we are trying to learn.

Do methods give your learners a chance to perform the new learning

Having Your Learners Do What You Want Them to Learn

You are providing your learners with an experience with the new skill when you have each one perform the skill. The nature of the skill will determine the **do** methods which are most appropriate. The most common **do** method is the worksheet. It provides the teacher with the opportunity to see if the learners know the right answers. Many skills cannot be performed on a worksheet because the answers only **describe** the skill. For these skills, the worksheet is not an appropriate **do** method.

You may want to teach your learners how to brush their teeth. After you have **told** them and **shown** them how to perform the skill, you will want to plan an activity for everyone to **do** the skill. That means that you will have to provide each learner with at least a toothbrush. Then you could plan role-playing, videotaping, photographs, a contest or a checklist. Using any one or several of these **do** methods, you provide your learners with an experience which has them practice brushing their teeth.

Repeat Exercise

You know how important it is for the learners to **repeat** the skill. And it is necessary for them to **repeat** it more than once. It would be helpful for you to answer the following question:

"How will my learners **repeat** the skill?"

In other words, what methods will you select to have the learners repeat the skill? You can use the list of methods below to find several **do** methods that the learners could use just to **repeat** the new skill. Remember that you will not want the learners to use more than one skill in the repeat exercise.

REPEAT METHODS

Chart
Collection
Committees
Contests
Creative Writing
Debate
Discussion
Exhibit
Fair
Forum
Games
Oral Report
Panel

Play
Poster Making
Projects
Questions
Reports
Research
Simulations
Skit
Story Telling
Tape Making
Transparency Making
Worksheets
Workshops

Others: _____   _____

_____   _____

_____   _____

_____   _____

Understanding How to Select Methods for Repeating

It is necessary for the learners to repeat the skill all by itself. This way they can concentrate fully on performing the skill steps of this new skill. Suppose the new skill was writing a complete sentence. Some methods that could be used for a repeat exercise are committees, contests, games, written questions, and worksheets. An example of a way to plan the repeat exercise would be to have the learners form committees (method) and to answer questions (method) on a worksheet (method) using complete sentences (skill). Note that the learners are just repeating that one skill. It would not be appropriate at this time to have the learners use creative writing as a method. They would have to use other skills such as writing a topic sentence and writing a paragraph as well as the new skill of writing complete sentences.

The simplest exercise is to have the learners **repeat** doing the skill.

Expanding Skill Repetitions within the Method

Once you have selected the repeat methods of the exercise, consider ways that the learners can repeat the skill within these methods. It would not be sufficient practice for the learners to write one sentence or print the letter "i" **once**, or add **one** example. You expand the repetitions within the method as carefully as you selected the method. You need to answer another question:

"How many different ways can my learners repeat the skill using the methods I have selected?"

You will write the examples or items that require the learners to repeat the new skill within the methods.

Examining the Parts of the Skill

To write the examples within the method, you should consider the parts that the learners will use when doing the skill. If the skill is writing a sentence, then the parts are all the words the learners know and can spell. If the skill is adding two-digit numbers to two-digit numbers, then the parts are numbers 10-99. If the skill is finding major U.S. cities on a map, then the parts are all major U.S. cities. When you know the parts that are the skill, then you can expand the ways that you have the learners repeat the skill. If you think how many words your learners know and can spell, then the number of sentences they can write for practice is almost limitless. Think how many practice examples you could write when you combine only two numbers from the ninety two-digit numbers available to you. To list the major U.S. cities, you need only turn to the index of an atlas to give your learners plenty of repeat practice.

When you expand ways to use the skill, you are increasing your repertoire of teaching methods.

Apply Exercises

After the learners have performed the skill in the repeat exercise, they will need to **apply** the skill. To write the **apply** exercises, you should answer the question, "What applications should my learners use to practice the skill?"

You will want to write the methods for practicing the applications. Choosing the methods used in **apply** exercises is accomplished in the same manner as choosing the repeat exercises. You will review the list of **apply** methods below with respect to the applications of the skill. If possible, try to select different apply methods. They will add variety to the learners' practice.

APPLY METHODS

Brainstorming	Panel
Case Study	Play
Collection	Poster Making
Colloquium	Practicum
Committees	Project
Contests	Psychodrama
Creative Writing	Questions
Current Events	Rating Scale
Debate	Reports
Exhibit	Research
Fair	Role Models
Forum	Simulations
Games	Skit
Hands-On Improvisation	Story Telling
Inventory	Survey
Laboratory	Worksheets
Model	Workshops
Oral Report	

Others: _____   _____

_____   _____

Understanding How to Select Apply Methods
for the Exercise

A very important aspect of writing apply exercises is to be certain that the learners have already mastered all the old skills they will be expected to use within the application. This ensures success with the task and mastery of the new skill. The learners will be confident of their performance and thus free to learn what you are teaching. When teaching the skill of writing a complete sentence, you could select writing a paragraph as an application if the learners have already learned how to write a paragraph. Some apply methods that could be used for applications are creative writing, current events, oral reports, and story telling. To practice the skill of writing complete sentences, the learners could write a paragraph (application) on a current events topic (method) and then give a brief oral report (method) speaking in complete sentences (skill).

Applications prepare your learners to use the new learning in life situations.

Expanding Application Repetitions within the Methods

Your goal is to have the learners perform the new skill as many times as possible. But you also want them to apply the new skill in as many different contexts as possible. To expand the applications within the method, you need to answer the following question:

"How many different ways can my learners apply the skill using the methods I have selected?"

As you write the apply exercises, you will expand the ways the learners can repeat the applications as well as the new skill.

Expanding the applications of a skill will add variety to your teaching.

Examining the Parts of the Application

You will identify the parts of your application to help you to expand the apply exercises. If the application is writing a paragraph, then the parts are the topic sentence, body, and summary sentence. If the application is buying items costing less than a dollar, then the parts are any items that cost less than a dollar. If the application is charting large U.S. city populations, then the parts are the different kinds of charts the learners can make.

Once you know these parts, you can expand the ways the learners apply the skill. When you think about how many different topics the learners can select in current events, the number of paragraphs expands tremendously. Simulating buying two items in a candy store would easily expand the number of repetitions of the apply exercises. Consider how many different ways the learners could use a list, or pictures, or bar graphs, or line graphs. When you break down all the parts of the applications, the choices increase the number of application exercises.

Summarizing Tell, Show, Do, Repeat, and Apply Methods

You have learned how to apply **tell**, **show**, **do** methods to the skill of the content. Then you have seen how **repeat** and **apply** exercises give additional practice with the skill steps. The principle difference between repeat and apply exercises is that **the learners use only the new skill when they repeat. When they apply the new skill, they practice it in conjunction with previously learned skills**. These methods are summarized by the following:

Tell You plan to have materials, other learners, a guest, or yourself **tell** the skill steps. The telling deals with words and may be oral or written.

Show You plan to have materials, other learners, a guest, or yourself **show** the skill steps. The showing uses images and may be a live demonstration or illustration.

Do You plan activities that allow all the learners to **do** the skill using the skill steps. The **doing** is an action on the part of the learners.

Repeat You select a method that has the learners use the new skill in isolation. Then consider the parts of the skill that can be used in different combinations to increase the repetitions of the skill.

Apply You choose an application that includes only those skills which your learners have already learned. Then select a method within which the application can be used for the learners' practice. Increase the number of exercises within the method by examining the different combinations possible from the parts of the application.

Maria spent several hours writing her first language arts lesson plan. After her first draft, she had an insight.

"Why, these are skills all the learners in my class should learn to do. Even though they have such different reading levels, they could all learn these skills."

Tapping her pencil beside the exercise of her lesson plan, she continued, "I just need to write four different exercises for my four reading groups. Then the learners can repeat and apply the new skill using reading materials that are appropriate for them."

Satisfied with her lesson plan for that all-important first day, Maria copied the plan into her journal.

Lesson Plan

Skill: *Describing the Setting of a Short Story in a Written Sentence*

Review: 1.   *Show learners a chart of the following steps:*   *(Tell)*

a.   *Study picture.*

b.   *Determine where the picture was taken.*

c.   *Determine when the picture was taken.*

d.   *Say: This picture was taken (where) in (when)*

2.   *Have a different learner read each step to the rest of the class while you show the first picture.*   *(Tell)*

3.   *Have other learners show how they would do each step with the picture.*   *(Show)*

4.   *Have all the learners write down the setting of another picture.*   *(Do)*

Overview: 1. Tell the class: If you describe the setting of (Tell)
a short story, then you will be able to antici-
pate what could happen in the story.

2. Give an example of a story set in the South (Show)
during the Civil War.

3. Have the students write down what they could (Do)
write a story about if the setting were on a
deserted beach in the summer.

Presentation: 1. Ask the learners to help develop the steps for (Tell)
describing the setting of a short story with
you. Write them on the chalkboard.

a. Read the story.

b. Determine where the story takes place.

c. Determine when the story takes place.

d. Write: The story takes place __(where)__ in
__(when)__.

2. Tell the learners that "where" means the geogra- (Tell)
phical description. It could be a specific
country or city. Generally, it could be in
the mountains or in the desert.

3. Tell the learners that "when" means past, (Tell)
present, or future.

4. Read the learners a paragraph that describes (Tell)
a setting. Have the different learners do
steps B, C, and D to show the rest of the class
how to use the steps.

5. Have one of the better readers read another (Do)
paragraph. All the learners should write a
sentence to describe the setting.

Exercise:	1.	Learners do a worksheet which has five para-	(Repeat)
		graphs from five different short stories.	
	2.	Learners read a short story and draw a picture	(Apply)
		of the setting.	
Summary:	1.	Have the learners write the steps in their	(Tell)
		notebooks.	
	2.	Ask a learner to show the class how to describe	(Show)
		the setting from an example in the exercise.	
	3.	Have all the learners practice once more on	(Do)
		another paragraph which a student reads to them.	

Writing Your Lesson Plans

At this point, you should take your daily content and write a lesson plan. The plan should include a ROPES organization. While checking over your lesson, be sure that you have planned how to **tell** and **show** the skill steps. The **do** methods should allow each learner a chance to perform the skill. Write five consecutive lesson plans to include in your journal.

LESSON PLAN   DATE: _____

SKILL: _____

REVIEW: _____

_____

_____

_____

_____

_____

OVERVIEW: _____

_____

_____

_____

_____

_____

75   **PRESENTATION:** _____

_____

_____

_____

_____

_____

EXERCISE: _____

_____

_____

_____

_____

_____

SUMMARY: _____

_____

_____

_____

_____

_____

While stacking the learning materials on her desk, Maria took a last look at her lesson plan. She felt good about the night's work and smiled to herself. It was going to be a great year! Sure, it was a little scary, too. To be responsible for twenty-eight kids was not to be taken lightly. Maria knew she had a lot of learning to do about those twenty-eight learners. Each one would be different but with many of the same needs.

"I'll spend my first week learning all I can about those kids," Maria thought. "Even this first lesson will give me an opportunity to see what my students can do." Again she looked over what she had written. "The review, overview, and presentation will give me some idea about the kids that like to participate verbally in class. During the exercise I'll have a chance to hear some of the learners read. And then I can get an idea of their writing skills after I collect and correct the exercise. That's neat! My students will be learning about the setting and I'll be learning about my characters!"

Using Maria's Experience

Have you ever considered your planning as a way to help you learn more about your learners? A class discussion can help you assess how well some of your learners understand new facts and concepts. If you plan a laboratory, some learners will demonstrate that they understand the principle of the new skill. Each time you plan a **do** method, you give the learners a chance to tell you what skills they can do and what they cannot do. You do not have to wait to give a formal test to learn more about your learners. Instead, you will respond to your learners as you deliver ROPES.

Diagnosing the Learners 3

Tossing aside the blankets, Maria thumped out of bed. Her alarm clock indicated that it was several minutes after midnight.

"I just can't sleep," she muttered as she wrapped herself in a robe. "I've got a good case of first-day jitters!"

After making her way to the kitchen, she measured a cup of milk into a saucepan. Then rummaging through the cabinets, she was able to find a nearly empty can of cocoa. She shook the tin to measure out the last of the powder. While the milk heated, Maria went over to the table and opened her briefcase. Taking out her plans she studied them closely.

"I've gone over these so many times I know them by heart," she sighed. Seated at the table with the hot cocoa, Maria ran through tomorrow morning in her mind.

"I'll be at the door to greet everyone as they come in. That will give me a chance to learn some names. These kids are too old for name tags so a seating chart should help me learn the rest of the names, I'll begin by introducing myself to the kids."

Maria had planned a ten-minute slide show to tell her class about herself. She had included pictures of her family, friends, neighborhood, activities, and her likes and dislikes. Then she had planned to tell the learners what her teaching goals were for the coming year. At that point she wanted the learners to help her develop some basic rules for the classroom. Once there were some rules. Maria would be able to get some input from her learners about themselves.

After draining the last drop of cocoa, Maria returned her plans to her briefcase. "My plans are good," she said to herself. Opening her closet door she reached in and pulled out her new first-day dress. The soft material of the skirt flared out as she swung it around in front of her. Turning in front of the mirror to catch her reflection she said, "The dress may look good but the face will look terrible if I don't get some rest!"

RESPONDING TO CONTENT

Palms sweaty, Maria shifted from one foot to the other as she stood at the door of the classroom. "This is it," she said as she peered down the long empty corridor. Behind her, the room was decorated brightly with colored construction paper and glossy photographs. Names of her new students were sprinkled over a bulletin board at the front of the room. She jumped as the metallic jangle of the opening bell cut the silence. From below she could hear the rush of children climbing the stairs, the sounds of footsteps punctuated by children's excited voices. In front of her stood a small girl staring up at her owlishly from behind the thickest glasses Maria had ever seen.

"Hi, Janet. I'm Miss Burbank, your new teacher."

Janet's face broke into a huge grin of surprise. "How'd 'cha know my name, huh? Miss Bur . . . Burbank."

"I remember you from Mrs. Snow's class," Maria explained.

By this time the doorway was full of children, elbowing their way toward Maria. A tall, slim boy had edged his way around the group to slip into the room unnoticed.

Maria called out, "Good Morning, Kenneth."

Head down, he mumbled something from behind her.

"Morning, Angela! Hello, John! Hi, Patrice!" Maria smiled trying to greet as many of her students by name as she could. And when she couldn't, she asked them their names.

The children milled around inside the room in groups of already established friends. Here and there a newcomer stood alone taking in the other children, sizing them up. And Maria, too.

And so the first day of school began for Maria. She had shown her slides in front of the seated children and had spoken with them about herself. The children liked that. Patrice nudged Theresa and looked approvingly at Maria. Even Kenneth shifted his gaze up once or twice from under the shock of hair that hid his eyes from the world.

"Since I've told you about me, I would like to know some things about all of you." Maria spread out her arms in a gesture to indicate the whole class. "But before we do that, we'll need some rules to follow in this class."

Several students groaned. Others deflated by several inches in their seats.

"She's just like all the rest," hissed a voice.

"You're telling me you don't like rules," responded Maria.

Several students looked surprised. Others exchanged glances.

"That's right!"

"That's why we don't like school. The rules take out all the fun."

"Yeah, who needs 'em!"

Five or six children clamored together in an increasing din.

Maria responded again to what the children were saying. "You're telling me you're not sure why there have to be rules in school."

The children began to all talk at once. No one could hear a word. Maria waited patiently until they had quieted. Then Tony spoke up.

"You guys are stupid! You're makin' all that noise and givin' me a headache. Ya gotta have some rules else someone's gonna get hurt."

Maria observed that Tony had some followers.

"He's right, man! Ya gotta have **some** rules."

"Yeah, like ya can't bring guns to school. Stuff like that."

More children reacted affirmatively and began shaking their heads up and down.

Maria used her responding skills again. "You mean, Tony, that we need rules to protect us."

Maria's responding skills opened the door for a spirited class discussion on rules. While the class had started off with only half their number as proponents of rules, nearly everyone wanted to give their view on the matter. Maria used Tony's reactions to establish the first classroom rule.

"During class discussions only one person can talk at a time."

"That's good, Miss Burbank. That way I won't get a headache listening to these idiots all babbling at once," Tony responded. All the students, some more grudgingly than others, had to agree that it was a necessary rule.

Learning to Attend to Your Learners[5]

You prepare to teach by **attending physically, observing, and listening.** Attending physically simply means communicating to the learners that you are ready to provide them with your full and undivided attention. Observing means being able to "see" the physical behaviors and characteristics of the learners which give you cues to their experience: instead of a crowd of youthful faces, you note a frown, a grin, a pair of eyes that follow you in bright anticipation. Listening means being able to "hear" what has been said and how it has been said in order to understand the learner's experience: instead of a babble of voices, you pick out this learner's calm and assured comment or that one's hesitant, almost embarrassed question. Attending skills set the stage for responding in two basic ways. First, when you signal to the learners that you are ready to give them your full and undivided attention, they are more likely to start exploring themselves in relation to the learning material. Second, attending skills serve to give you all the cues you need to deliver your best responses which, in turn, set the stage for making you an effective teacher.

[5]For more information on attending skills, see the Reference section.

Learning Responding Skills

Responding is really the first stage of interpersonal skills. Responding means communicating an understanding of the experience expressed by the learners: "You're really excited about all the things you saw on your vacation, aren't you?" Responding facilitates the learners' exploration of where they are in relation to themselves, you, the learning material, or their worlds in general. Responding lays the base for personalizing the learner's understanding.

Teacher: Interpersonal   Attending   Responding
            Skills

Learner: Learning Skills   Exploring

Learning to Respond to Your Learners[6]

Attending, observing, and listening behaviors make responding behavior possible. And responding behavior makes it possible for the learner to explore where she or he is, both in relation to her or himself and in relation to the learning material being presented. Until you share an awareness of how the learner's feel about the learning and why they feel that way, neither of you can make progress. Your accurate response reflects your understanding, and helps them to explore more fully. Minimally effective responses are high on responsiveness, or the communication of understanding, and low on initiative, or the communication of direction and guidance. Such high-low responses are interchangeable with the learner's responses. They capture the feeling and the reason for the feeling that the learners have expressed. In other terms, the teacher has expressed essentially the same message that the learners have communicated to her. We can compare the teacher's response to the learner's responses and agree that they are essentially identical in terms of the experience expressed by the learners.

Responsive behavior, in turn, lays the base for effective initiative behavior by giving us the understanding we need to provide guidance and direction. Responding to the learners assures them that we know where they are. The learners will be more open to the direction and guidance that we provide when they are certain that we understand where they are.

You will begin by responding to content. More simply, that means you will find a way of expressing what the learners have said. This will give your learners an opportunity to hear what they have said and to tell you whether or not that is what they meant.

When you respond to content you will say: You're saying   (the gist)   or I hear you saying   (the gist)

[6]For more information on responding to content, see the References Section.

Practicing Responding to the Learner's Content

You should practice writing responses to typical learner statements. Remember that you are just letting the learners know that you have heard what they said correctly. Do not initiate or give advice. Once you can write responses to content you can practice these skills with your friends, professors, and students. You can increase your communication competence.

Learner Expression 1:   Those kids are always so mean to me. They think they're so good!

_____

_____

_____

Learner Expression 2:   You're always pickin' on me. It's not jes' me that's doin stuff.

_____

_____

_____

Learner Expression 3:   That sure was fun today . . . playin' that math game. We never done things like that before.

_____

_____

_____

There were two principles that Maria had learned about responding to her learners' content. The first was that responding to what her learners were saying helped her learn more about them. She had encouraged her learners to present themselves more fully to her as they told her what they really thought about rules. Maria had started her diagnosis of these twenty-eight individuals.

Secondly, Maria found that her responding skills could be used to defuse student-teacher confrontations. As the learners heard Maria repeat their meaning, they realized that this teacher was listening to what they said. Instead of shocking their new teacher, she had listened and understood what they were saying.

This is what Maria wrote in her journal after the first day and the discussion of rules:

> Teaching was fun today! I'm going to love those kids. Yes, it was a good day even though I had my moments of doubt. Like the discussion on rules. If it hadn't been for the responding skills I learned in Ed. 202, I would have lost them. Instead, I found out quite a bit about kids. I found out that Manny likes to challenge authority. He isn't particular about who he challenges. It seems to be his way of getting attention. He certainly got my attention when he said he hated school because of all the rules. Patrice and Theresa want to please. They like rules. Tony is the natural leader in the class, although Manny would like to be.

Using Maria's Experience

Have you ever thought to use responding skills to diagnose your learners? Probably not. Of course you plan to diagnose your learners with tests. But the learners will tell you many things about themselves if you listen. By repeating the gist of what they say, you help these learners add depth to that diagnosis.

In addition, you should try to respond to the learners who are potential problems in the classroom. A teacher can always gain the upper hand by sending the students to the office or assigning dictionary work. When you choose to pull rank on your students, you establish a pattern for the same behavior to happen again. Responding to the problems of the learners can prevent that problem from occurring again. The learner with that problem has heard you respond to a behavior, not with retaliation but with understanding.

Maria was finishing up the presentation of her language arts lesson. Her students were having varying degrees of success in writing a sentence to describe the setting. As she walked among the students, she checked their work.

Maria walked by Manny's desk and paused. Manny shrugged his shoulders and mumbled, "How's it look? Am I doin' it right?"

Examining his work, she said, "Let me look at what you've written, Manny. You've said, 'This story takes place in California.' " Maria paused and handed Manny his paper.

He scowled for a minute and then looked up at Maria with understanding. "I left out a step . . . the third step. I gotta tell when the story took place, right, Miss Burbank?"

Smiling, Maria said, "That's right, Manny. It's important to follow all the steps." Then she moved on to Patrice's desk.

Patrice's tightly braided head bent industriously over her work. "Can I see what you've written, Patrice?" questioned Maria as she leaned down to get a better look at the paper.

Turning her head, Patrice looked at Maria nervously. "I think I did it right. I followed the steps, kind of." Gathering her courage together she read from the paper. **"The Rush for Gold** takes place in California in 1849."

Maria responded to Patrice's content. "You're not really sure that you did the steps correctly, Patrice."

"Well, I did the steps right except for the fourth step. I added to that one." Patrice seemed to gather confidence as she discussed her answer with Maria. "I named the story. You didn't tell us to actually write the name of the story." Her large brown eyes studied Maria's face for a reaction.

"You not only followed the steps but you improved on them. That was good thinking, Patrice! You have learned a new skill today." Patrice breathed a visible sigh of relief as Maria moved on to the last desk.

John twitched in his seat, averting his head so as not to look at Maria. On his paper was written in smudges:

Maria knew that John had a poor reading level. So she responded to the work that he had done. "You're not really sure how to follow these steps, John."

John shrugged his shoulders and shuffled his feet on the floor. "Uh, I guess so."

Then Maria asked John to read the steps. That way she could diagnose if his reading was holding him back. Haltingly he managed to read the four steps. Maria responded, "You've just told me you can read the steps, John."

"Yeah, I can read 'em. But I don't know the where and when stuff."

For the first time, John looked Maria fully in the eye, studying her closely to see if she would laugh at him. Maria returned his searching look with a steady gaze. Pulling up a chair, she began to explain the supportive knowledge that John needed in order to complete the steps.

What Maria had done with Manny, Patrice, and John was to use her responding skills to help diagnose their problems with respect to the learning content. She responded to what her learners said about their learning. She responded to what her learners did with their learning. That evening she was able to reflect on how she used these responding skills as she wrote in her journal.

> Maybe I can help Manny to become that leader. All he needed today was some responding from me to help him diagnose what steps he had left out of his statement. Patrice was worried that I wouldn't approve of the extra effort she put into doing her skill. Mrs. Snow probably threw a fit last year if the kids didn't do exactly as she said. I'm glad that I was able to reassure her that she had done the skill correctly.

> Responding even helped me work with John. If I hadn't taken the time to find out what his problem was, he'd still be sitting there with two words on his paper. Instead I was able to help him understand what "where" and "when" meant. That vital supportive knowledge was missing for him. Without that, he was unable to do the skill.

Using Maria's Experience

When you teach your learners, use your responding skills to diagnose if your learners can perform the skill. This is the starting point for your content diagnosis. Sometimes the students' behaviors will indicate a problem with the content. You will respond to the eyes staring vacantly into space by saying: "Janet, are you having trouble finding the first word in your dictionary?"

In most cases your learners will be more direct about their inability to perform the skill.

"Miss Burbank, I don't get this stuff at all. Can you help me?" Then you can begin your responding by diagnosing that the learners cannot perform the skill.

Your next level of diagnosis wll be to respond to determine which skill steps your learners can and cannot perform. Again, you may have to encourage input from your learners by saying, "Show me how you would do the first step, Janet." Janet's response will determine if she has problems with the first step.

More often your learners will be able to tell you, if you ask them, what steps they can do and what steps they cannot do.

"I can do everything except this last step, Miss Burbank." With their responses, you have made the second level diagnosis. You have diagnosed what skill they cannot perform and which skill steps they are missing which keep them from performing.

You will have to respond to diagnose the supportive knowledge that is preventing your learners from succeeding with the skill steps. They may not grasp the principle of when to use the skill.

"I don't see any reason why I need to learn this," one student may say.

A concept used in a skill step may be a problem for some of your learners.

"I don't know what 'vibrating' means," another may say.

Others may not know the facts of the skill steps.

"What is a 'pipette'?" a learner may ask.

Your responding skills will help you diagnose these learners when they cannot ask you the right question. As you respond, you will find your learners using your response to diagnose themselves.

RESPONDING TO FEELING

Maria glanced up at the large clock on the wall and said aloud, "Whoops! I almost forgot recess." All the children packed up. Some showed their pleasure non-verbally with smiles and waves. Others sang out their expressions of pleasure.

"Oh, boy!"

"It's about time!"

"Be on my team, Tony?"

"I'm ready!"

The children rushed to line up at the door. A tangle of arms and legs pushing and shoving jammed the doorway. Several yelps of pain and anger issued from injured parties.

"Everyone sit down again," stated Maria in a matter-of-fact voice. The children returned to their seats, some reluctantly, others with embarrassment and still others nursing minor bruises.

"Some of you feel angry," responded Maria looking at those who were most eager to be out the door. Angry scowls began to disappear, replaced by guarded expressions.

Maria turned to another group and said, "Some of you feel embarrassed." Patrice and Theresa hung their heads looking at one another sideways.

Then Maria looked at John and Janet and said, "Some of you feel hurt." Both students nodded their heads vigorously as they continued to rub their bruises.

Maria looked at the children seriously. "I think we need another rule to protect us, don't you?" Most heads nodded up and down, some more reluctantly than others. "That means no yelling, running, or pushing when you line up," continued Maria with concern. Then she smiled. "You all feel anxious about missing more of your recess, right?"

The anger, embarrassment, and hurt disappeared. Once again the children were back with Maria as they all said, "YES!"

"So let's go," said Maria as she gestured toward the door. And this time the children lined up with order and purpose. At the head of the line, Maria looked down the ranks of her learners. "Now, you make **me** feel proud!"

Determining How Your Learners Feel[7]

Understanding how a person feels is the most important part of understanding where he or she is. In order to respond to feelings, we must do several things. First, we must know what a feeling word is. Feeling words refer directly to feelings such as happy, sad, or mad. Sometimes you may use a word or phrase which describes a situation in a figurative sense, such as "You feel like climbing the walls," which represents feeling bored or alone, even though the individual may be surrounded by people. In order to determine the appropriate feeling word, you must use all the attending behaviors which you have learned. You must attend fully to the learner; you must observe the learner's behavior, particularly his or her facial expressions which give us cues to feelings; you must listen to the learner's voice because his or her tone of voice will also give us cues to feelings. You must listen to the learner's words. Then you can ask how he or she has related to you, using behavioral cues and words together to decide the appropriate word. It is most important that you initially suspend your own frame of reference. Ignore the apparent irrationality of Thomas' rage; don't linger over thoughts like "He shouldn't feel that way." The goal is simply to understand what the learner is saying and how he or she feels about it.

We will use the reflective format, *"You feel _____."* This format provides a structure which insures delivery. You can check yourself out to determine whether, in fact, you have delivered an accurate response to the student's experience. You can do a lot of good teaching with this format even though it may seem stereotyped. Master the skills before you work on individualizing your delivery.

---

[7]For more information on responding to feeling, see the References sections.

Responding to Feeling in the Classroom

You can respond to the feelings of a large group of learners in the classroom. Try to identify the feelings they are expressing by asking yourself how their experiences would make you feel. At a minimum, make gross discriminations about whether your learners are feeling "up" or "down." Then respond to them, using feeling words that reflect their "good" or "bad" feelings. A gang of boys in one corner, supposedly working on a group project, are laughing and talking excitedly. You might respond "Well, you guys sure feel full of life today!" By responding accurately, you can account for the important feeling dimensions of the entire group's learning experience. And you will prepare the group for exploring the meaning or reason for the feeling.

When you respond to the feelings of your learners, you help them explore.

Practicing Responding to the Learners' Feelings

Next you need to practice writing a response to typical learner feelings. You want your learners to know that you understand them so well that you even know how they feel. Do nothing more than identify those feelings. Formulate your response by using the format, "You feel _____."
Once you can correctly discern the learners' feelings from written examples, try to use this additional responding skill with your friends and students as they show their feelings.

Learner Expression 4: I hate doing this stupid stuff. I always get it wrong!

_____

Learner Expression 5: I made the team! I can't believe it! I never thought I'd do it!

_____

Learner Expression 6: I'm gonna really miss my Dad. We always had a lot of fun. But not anymore!

_____

Maria spent an active fifteen minutes on the playground with her class. Most of the boys and a very few girls were engaged in a free-for-all soccer game. The players yelled and ran in waves up and down the pavement after the black-and-white ball. First one way, then the other.

"I hope no one gets hurt in that mess," shuddered Maria. "They certainly are enjoying the exercise, though," she observed looking at their enthusiastic faces.

Then she looked around at the rest of the girls. They hung around talking in groups of two or three. "What a shame that these kids can't run around, too. I want to get them in on some of that fun."

Taking two soccer balls, Maria called to the groups of girls, "Let me show you some of the things I know about soccer."

Hesitantly, the girls circled around Maria. "Come on Angela, Barbara. Over here."

First she told them and then showed them how to dribble the ball. Then she had each girl dribble the ball while she watched. Finally, it was Angela's turn.

"Aw, please, Miss Burbank. I don't wanna do that. I'll look like a jerk!"

"You feel stupid dribbling the ball, Angela," responded Maria.

Angela looked up at Maria with surprise. "Yeah, that's right! I feel stupid 'cause I look stupid!"

Barbara joined in. "Aw c'mon, Angi. We won't laugh at you. You don't look no more stupid than we do." With that, Barbara took a ball and stumbled after it as it zigzagged crazily across the playground.

Angela smiled as she watched her friend Barbara. "I can do it better than that," she shouted. Grabbing the second ball, she dribbled unevenly after Barbara as Maria watched.

Those kids sure can be a handful! They were so mad at me for holding them back at recess. It took all my self-control not to shriek at them for their unruly behavior. Responding to their feelings really helped me diagnose their problem. They were just jumping out of their skins to get some exercise. I'll have to remember that tomorrow. Maybe I can figure out some way for them to move around and stretch before recess.

I hope I can give those girls the skills they need for playground. They've just never had a chance to practice with a ball. All of them felt awkward and self-conscious about their lack of skill. If I can get them to practice regularly, maybe they'll feel better about playing games. After all, kids are made for motion. Some just never get a chance!

Responding to your learners' feelings can add valuable dimensions to your diagnosis of their strengths and weaknesses. Like Maria, you will draw conclusions as you watch their reactions to your responses. You can check out if your learners feel embarrassed or happy or angry about the skills they are doing. They may feel good or confused or mad about the skill step they can or cannot do. The supportive knowledge may make them feel confident or confused or lost. Your learners' feelings are a reaction to what happens in your classroom. They are your cues to find a meaning for these feelings. Use them as a signpost toward that diagnosis.

RESPONDING TO FEELING AND MEANING

Maria's students trooped in from the playground and up the wide staircase to their second floor classroom. The recess had given them a charge of energy which showed in their quick strides and straight shoulders. The line rambled a bit behind Maria. Every once in a while their good spirits bubbled out of their mouths. Maria had to turn to "shush" them with a finger at her lips. Inside the room, most students found their seats. Tony and Manny lingered by the tall windows comparing notes on the soccer game. Angela and Barbara were being teased by John in the back of the room. Maria approached them.

"You're telling me that you aren't ready to begin working," responded Maria to the three students.

The three students turned to face Maria.

"Miss Burbank," said Angela trying to explain. "John says we'll never be able to play soccer. We will, won't we?"

"Yeah, Miss Burbank. Tell him," chimed in Barbara.

Maria looked intently at the two girls. "You want to be able to play soccer."

"We sure do," answered Angela.

Barbara nodded her head in agreement.

"You're upset with John." Maria continued to respond, this time to their feelings.

"All he can do is make fun of us," scowled Angela.

"We're gonna learn!" added Barbara.

"You feel upset because you want to be able to play soccer and John is making fun of you." This time, Maria responded to their feeling and meaning.

Both girls agreed that it was unfair of John to tease them. "He's not gonna stop us, Miss Burbank," affirmed Angela. "We're not too good now, but we're gonna practice."

Responding to Feeling and Meaning[8]

Responding to how the person feels is critical but it is also incomplete. To communicate a complete understanding of what the learners are saying, you also have to recognize the meaning of their statements. Meaning is the reason for the feeling. Meaning is a combination of the feeling and the content. When responding to the meaning, do not simply repeat the content of what the learners have said; rather, attempt to capture and express the personal reason for the feeling. Let us look at the following illustration of an expression by an elementary school child.

"They're always picking on me! You know, ganging up on me and pushing me around. I don't even want to go to school anymore."

Here the teacher's response might be as follows:

"You feel scared because they might really hurt you."

The "might really hurt you" part of the teacher's response supplies the learner's reason for the feeling. It summarizes the meaning in a personal way rather than just repeating the content.

Learning the Reason for the Feeling

Responding to meaning, then, is simply providing the reason for the feeling. Here are several more illustrations that might help you learn this skill.

"You feel sad because the teacher didn't pick you."

"You feel angry because the teacher didn't even think about you."

"You feel happy because the teacher made you captain of the team."

Each of these three illustrations relates to the teaching situation. In each illustration, the reason for the feeling (the meaning) is used to complement the feeling response.

[8]For more information on responding to feeling and meaning, see the References section.

Making Feeling and Meaning Responses

Responding accurately to the learners facilitates their exploration of where they are. At a minimum, the teacher is able to communicate some understanding of the learners to the learners. When you think about it, that's really not too much to expect: to be at least able to understand the learners at the level at which they have presented themselves. To be able to recognize young Brad's problem, for example, by attending to him physically, observing his tear-streaked face and woeful expression, listening to his words and tone of voice; and to be able to respond to him accurately and fully by using a vocabulary of feeling terms that he can recognize. Indeed, there can be no effective teaching without this kind of response!

Practice Responding to Learners' Expressions

You can respond to feeling and meaning in the classroom. First pick out the children with whom you think you have a relationship. By starting with the learners with whom you have the best relationship, you build in success for yourself and for them. Leave the learners whom you are having difficulty reaching until later. This way you will have more mastery of the skills when you come to them. In general, move from the learners with whom you have the best relationship to those with whom you have the poorest relationship. Next, find or create an opportunity to respond to the learners using the format *"You feel_____ because_____."* Do not forget your attending, observing, and listening skills. Be sure to note their reactions to your response. They should go on to talk more about where they are in relation to themselves, to you, or to the learning material. In some way, they should acknowledge that you have reached them.

Next, increase the number of students to whom you will respond. Increase by one per day the number of learners you are responding to until you are responding to at least fifteen to twenty different learners each day. As you start to build a number of responses each day, you may want to begin to vary the format. Here are some alternatives: *"It feels _____ when _____."* Or, *"You're feeling _____ when _____."* Or, *"You feel like _____ because _____."* Do not use *"You feel that _____."* This format is always less effective because it tends to emphasize only what happened and not how the learner feels.

Now respond to each learner you have in cycles of fifteen to twenty. If you have thirty students, each learner should be responded to at an average of every other day. If you have 150 students, each learner should receive a response at least once every ten days. Evidence indicates that this responsiveness alone will make a significant difference in the responsive atmosphere of your classroom and thus in the achievement and growth of your learners.

When you respond, you help your learners grow.

Responding in the Classroom

You can respond to both feeling and meaning for a large group of learners in the classroom. You make gross discriminations about whether the class or groups of learners are feeling "good" or "bad." Then you identify the reasons for these feelings. For example, your learners may be feeling positive and optimistic because they all passed a recent test with flying colors. In such a situation, of course, the reason for their collective "up" feeling is their excellent performance. Here you might respond to feeling and meaning with a statement like, "You all feel glad because the test turned out to be so easy!" You can communicate your understanding to the entire group of learners in your feeling and meaning response.

When you respond, your learners know you understand them.

When you respond fully in the classroom, you combine your responses to feeling and meaning. Try to repeat verbatim or repeat the gist of the expressions that the learners have made. With groups of learners, you may want to attempt to categorize the topics or the content of the expression. For example, in relation to the learning tasks, do the expressions have to do with subjects, activities, or materials? Look for any common themes that you might hear, especially those that are repeated by different learners or different groups of learners. Then identify the feelings and the reason for the feelings and communicate your understanding to your entire group of learners. That way your learners will be able to explore where they are in relation to the learning tasks. And you will eventually be able to personalize their understanding of their explorations.

Consider the interactions between learners as well as those between you and the learners. Respond to feeling and meaning on a regular basis. Try to make sure that you respond accurately to each learner at least once every week or two. Many children have never had their experiences responded to accurately in their entire lifetimes. The principle of reciprocal effect will work for you in facilitating the learners' responsiveness to you and your teaching efforts. Indeed, later on you may want to teach them directly how to respond in learning.

Practicing Responding to the Learners' Feeling and Meaning

You have already practiced responding to the content and the feeling of different learners' expressions. These expressions are used as stimuli in the following exercise. Practice responding to the feeling and meaning of these six expressions. As you practice, you will want to ask yourself if you included a feeling word and a reason for the feeling. One way to do this is to use the format: "You feel _____ because _____." Then when you communicate with your students or friends you will be able to: 1) respond to their content, 2) respond to their feeling, and 3) respond to their feeling and meaning.

Learner Expression #1: Those kids are always so mean to me. They think they're so good!

_____

Learner Expression #2: You're always pickin' on me. It's not jes' me that's doin' stuff.

_____

Learner Expression #3: That sure was fun today . . . playin' that math game. We never done things like that before.

_____

Learner Expression #4:   I hate doing this stupid stuff. I always get it wrong.

_____

Learner Expression #5:   I made the team! I can't believe it! I never thought I'd do it!

_____

Learner Expression #6:   I'm gonna really miss my Dad. We always had a lot of fun. But not anymore!

_____

Everyone settled into their seats ready to begin. Maria divided the students into four groups based on their reading levels. Then she passed out the appropriate reading materials to each group. The aroma of fresh dittos filled the room. Some children pressed their papers to their noses to savor the familiar smell before it evaporated.

The groups were all practicing the same skill: describing the setting of a short story. Theresa bent over her paper to carefully sign her name on the smooth, fresh sheet. She straightened up to assess her efforts. Although her printing was fine by most standards, Theresa scowled to herself and erased letters. Then, blowing on her paper, she bent again to print still better letters. Tony hurriedly signed his paper and immediately focused on the task. Maria smiled as she realized that his goal was to be the first one done. After giving directions to the first three groups, Maria called the five poorest readers over to the round table in the back of the room.

"Kenneth, Janet, John, Nina, Luis. Bring your papers and a pencil."

Maria looked around the table and saw John trying to control his twitching by holding on tightly to the seat of his chair. Beside him, Janet smiled up at Maria with her eyes obscured behind the shimmering glasses. Kenneth kept his eyes on the floor while Nina and Luis watched Maria nervously. As Maria explained the directions, the students seemed to relax a tiny bit. Janet volunteered to read aloud first. Maria had typed Janet's paper on the special typewriter with large type. Yet Janet held her paper up until it almost touched her nose. Slowly she began to read one word at a time. Maria began her diagnosis, using a checklist as she listened to Janet read. She noted that Janet needed phrasing skills and word attack skills.

"Thank you, Janet. That was fine. You didn't forget how to read over the summer, did you?"

"Naw, but I wish I didn't have to be in this dummy group!"

Maria responded to Janet's content. "You would rather be back with the rest of the class."

Shaking her head dejectedly, Janet answered dully, "Yeah."

John joined in, "Can we go back with the rest of the class, uh, uh, Miss . . . ?" John's voice trailed off. Nina and Luis picked up the theme to tell Maria that they didn't like it either. Kenneth remained mute, staring at his paper.

Again Maria responded, this time to the students' feelings. "You all feel sad." She made eye contact with all except Kenneth who kept his eyes down.

"It's no fun always being in the low group," added Janet in a tone of voice that told Maria that she felt very sorry for herself.

Now Maria responded to the students' feelings and meaning. "It makes you sad because you have to be in the low group."

Janet, John, Nina, and Luis exchanged glances with each other in agreement.

Maria had responded to the group's content, feeling, and meaning. These skills had helped her make a diagnosis about these five students. She knew how they felt about being in the low group. They hated it!

This was going to be Maria's first major hurdle to overcome in her classroom. She had to help these students understand that they had too many missing skills to attempt to do the work the rest of the class was doing. They would need to understand that Maria could supply missing skills and skill steps. For if she was their teacher, she was there to help.

Using Maria's Experience

As you can see, Maria used her responding skills to make two different kinds of diagnoses. First, she diagnosed their intellectual responses to the learning material.

"Could they do the skill and skill steps?"

"Did they know the facts, concepts, and principles?"

Her second kind of diagnosis involved the students' emotional responses to the learning material.

"Were they afraid to try?"

"Did they hate the activity?"

"Were they proud of their work?"

When you respond to your learners, you should be making the same kind of diagnoses. You should ask yourself these three questions as you respond:

"What can my learners **do**?"

"What do my learners **know**?"

"How do my learners **feel**?"

I never thought I'd make it to the end of the day. Sometimes I thought I was learning too much about the kids. I mean. . .what do you say to Angela about being able to play soccer. The poor kid has two left feet. But she really wants to. . .I found that out. So I'll do all I can to help her.

Then there was Janet's reading group. I knew they hated being in that low group. But then when they told me how they felt, it was so much worse! My first instinct was to abolish the groups, right then. That was until I realized that abolishing the groups wasn't going to help the kids any. Sure, they might feel better for a day or two. But what happens when they can't do what the others do and they don't know what the others know? I've got to find another way to help them!

That's probably why teachers don't really ever get to know their students. Man! It's scary! Once you know it, what do you do about it?

Setting the Learners' Goals 4

PERSONALIZING THE MEANING

Maria smoothed the red checked table cloth over the extended table. "I really should be planning instead of entertaining," she thought guiltily. It was the Saturday night after the first three days of school. The gang wanted to get together to swap war stories. Of course, Maria had volunteered to cook. Setting eight places, she moved efficiently between the table and the kitchen. Then she made a last-minute check. The pot of water was boiling, filling the kitchen with steam. A large package of spaghetti waited on the counter. Maria lifted the cover of the sauce to taste the ingredients one last time. Satisfied, she replaced the cover just as a knock sounded on the door.

"It's us," called Lynn. Maria opened the door and Lynn hugged her. "This is Paul, Maria. I told you about this dude who teaches across the hall from me. . . well . . . here he is."

Maria extended her hand and said with mock confidentiality, "Come on in, Paul. Our password tonight is 'teaching'!"

Maria had just served Lynn and Paul some Chianti when the others arrived. The room filled with bits and pieces of conversation as groups of two and three talked about their week. Maria was too busy running back and forth to the kitchen to do anything but catch snatches of conversation.

" . . . and then this huge kid comes up to me . . . "

"So what was I supposed to do? The kid's barfing all over the . . . "

Lynn appeared at Maria's elbow. "Hey, let me help you. You look a bit frazzled."

Together they served the food and called everyone to the table. Lynn looked around the table and said, "Listen to what happened to me my very first day. Tell me what you guys would have done." The focus of the table turned to Lynn as she began her story.

"My class isn't bad. I mean it. But there's this one kid . . . Douglas, who's such a nudge. I mean the kid is smart but his mouth is always going. First I listened to him tell me how I should do things. Then I told him I was going to do things my way." Lynn held her head with both hands to exaggerate her frustration. "Then do you know what that kid did . . . he began to bawl. I mean it! What a mess! The other kids were laughing at this little freak crying and I was standing there with my mouth open. I couldn't believe it!"

"So what did you do?" questioned Maria.

Lynn laughed nervously, "I changed the subject. What else could I have done?"

Paul frowned and added, "You really could have helped the kid understand things a little better, Lynn. Maybe you could have taken him aside and explained your reasons for doing things."

"Better still," joined in Maria, "You could have responded to him. Then he could hear what he was telling you and you might have found out why it was so important for him to be so bossy."

Maria turned to Paul and began to role-play. "You're telling me, Douglas, that I should pass out the books now."

Paul picked up his cue. "Well, last year our teacher always passed out the books the very first thing."

"You feel upset, Douglas."

"Well, kinda. . ."

Maria responded to his feeling and meaning. "Douglas, you're upset because I'm not doing things like last year's teacher did."

"Yeah, you're doing everything different."

"It bothers you because you don't know what's coming next." This time Maria personalized the meaning.

"I might not do the right thing. I might do it wrong," responded Paul and Douglas.

"Oh, I know what you're doing," interrupted Lynn. "That's the stuff we learned in Dr. Adams' seminar . . . interpersonal skills."

You learn to personalize so that you can understand your learners — and so you can help them take control of their own lives and problems. In this context, personalizing to understand simply means that the teacher uses her own experience to help the learners to determine where they are in relation to where they want to go. Without an understanding of where they want to go, no goals may be developed. Without an understanding of where they want to go, no effective action program to achieve the goals is possible. Teacher personalizing facilitates the learners' understanding of where they are in relation to where they want to be.

Teacher: Interpersonal   Attending   ▶   Responding   Personalizing
             Skills   ▽   ↗   ▽

Students: Learning Skills   Exploring   Understanding

Personalizing Understanding

Attending and responding make understanding possible. In the context of a responsive base, personalizing skills enable the teacher to help the learners to understand where they are in relation to where they want to go. We will call those teacher responses that help the learners to understand where they are in relation to where they want to be **personalized understanding responses**. They go beyond what the learners have expressed themselves. The responses add to their own understanding of themselves. These personalized responses, in turn, lay the base for developing programs to get the learners from where they are to where they want to be. Understanding where the learners want to be helps to establish the goal of the program. Understanding where the learners are helps to establish the first step in the program.

When you personalize, you help your learners to understand themselves.

Personalizing our Responses

Now we will build a responsive base in class. Practice responding with feeling and meaning responses to learners for an extended period of time. As before, be sure to start with learners with whom you have a good relationship. Start by making two feeling and meaning responses and work your way up, one response at a time, to six or more responses. As you build the length of the interaction, it may be more appropriate to respond to learners outside the normal classroom interaction.

It is often difficult to do anything with expressions about third parties or situations. Learners often blame their parents or friends or teachers or some material like a test for their current predicament. And yet you may not be able to do anything about any of these other people or things. One approach available to you is to personalize your response to the learners. By personalizing your response, we mean involving the learners directly in their expression of their experience. By personalizing your response, you make the learners responsible directly for the feeling and meaning which they have expressed. In this way, you help them assume control.

Personalizing Meaning[9]

Your personalized response should clearly pinpoint the learners' part of their own experience. You want to put the focus upon them. You want to make the learners responsible or accountable for their part in the experience. The format that you can use to do this most effectively is as follows: *"You feel_____ because you_____."*

The first step is to ask, given the experience which has been expressed, what is the learner's role? How is the learner responsible? The answer to this question will provide the personalized reason for the feeling.

[9]For more information on personalizing meaning, see the References sections.

Practicing Personalizing the Learners' Meaning

Maria personalized Douglas' meaning when she said, "It bothers you because you don't know what's coming next." She knows Douglas is upset or bothered. That is how he feels about doing things differently from last year. Now she wants to point up his role in the situation by stating that he does not know what is going to happen next.

It will take some practice for you to learn how to personalize your learners' meanings. Begin by doing the exercises below. Write your response to the content of the initial stimulus expression. Then write hypothetical student responses as you respond to feeling and meaning. Then personalize the learner's meaning. Once you can write interpersonal responses, you should practice with your learners and friends.

Learner's Expression #1:   With dismay: *"Look at my plant! It's dead! Nothing ever works for me."*

Respond to Content: _____

_____

Learner's Response: _____

Respond to Feeling: _____

_____

Learner's Response: _____

Respond to Feeling and Meaning: _____

_____

Learner's Response: _____

Personalize the Meaning: _____

Learner's Expression #2:   With elation: *"I can't believe this report card. It's the best one I've ever gotten!"*

Respond to Content: _____

Learner's Response: _____

Respond to Feeling: _____

Learner's Response: _____

Respond to Feeling and Meaning: _____

Learner's Response: _____

Personalize the Meaning: _____

"That was a great meal, Maria," complimented Paul, getting up to take his dishes into the kitchen. The others followed until the table was cleared for dessert.

"Oh, that chocolate cake looks yummy," exclaimed Lynn to Peggy who was sitting beside her. "All those calories . . . but I've earned them after this week!"

Peggy grinned, "Haven't we all! I never thought I'd make it through the week. But somehow Friday came and I discovered that I was finding out a lot about the kids in my class."

Peggy included the whole table in her dialogue. "My kids are older than most of yours, but I don't think that makes much difference. Responding helped me diagnose my kids, just like you, Maria. My biggest problem, I find, is to help the kids understand it isn't the world that's wrong."

Maria smiled in agreement. "How true! Those kids just don't want to lose face in front of their teacher or the other kids. It must be the book's fault or the teacher must have the wrong answer. They couldn't have done it wrong."

"That's where I found personalizing helps me," continued Peggy. "As I'm working with the kids, I can diagnose what their strengths and weaknesses are with my responding skills. Then my personalizing skills help me prescribe what they need in order to succeed."

The conversation of the table swirled around Maria as she became lost in thought. "Poor Kenneth. He was just beginning to crawl out of his shell after the first few days of school. I didn't expect his group to have any problems with the math review. Then I heard him swearing under his breath at last year's teacher because he couldn't do any of the examples.

" 'You feel pretty angry because Mrs. Snow didn't teach you this subtraction, Kenneth.' He agreed readily. After all, it wasn't his fault. But then I had to personalize for him so that he would begin to understand what he had to learn.

" 'You feel angry because you don't know how to regroup hundreds and tens when you subtract.' Now it was my turn to decide how I would teach Kenneth the skill he needed to learn. I had made my diagnosis that Kenneth didn't know any of the skill steps. I would have to decide how to **tell**, **show**, **do** these skill steps."

Using Maria's Experience

Your teaching delivery benefits from two functions of personalizing. One of these functions helps your learners understand what their role is with respect to the situation. They cannot stop the external forces that seem to be causing their problem. If the test is too hard for Susie and Tom, then they need to understand what they can do about difficult tests. If another student is mean to Bill, then he can be helped to understand how he can deal with the meanness. In other words, you will help the learners internalize the situation in order to determine their role in that situation.

The other function of personalizing is for you, the teacher. Using the diagnosis, you begin to formulate how to present what the students need to learn. You plan to personalize that presentation for the individual, small group, or the whole class. Mary may need to read the skill steps as well as hear them because she takes so much time to ponder directions. In planning methods that are appropriate for these learners, you will think of examples that are relevant for your learners. John, for instance, has always lived in a rural environment so he will relate to examples about a farm. As you personalize, you prepare your learners to learn more effectively and yourself to teach more effectively.

Monday morning dawned crisp and cold. Maria shivered in her bare feet on the cold, kitchen floor as she waited for her morning coffee to perk. "I certainly feel different about starting this week," she thought to herself, recalling the first-day butterflies of last week. She had spent yesterday reviewing her lesson plans for the week. It had been necessary to rewrite some of the plans because of what she had learned about her students the first three days of school.

Maria entered school a half hour early. She had some extra math practice exercises to run off on the ditto for Kenneth's group. Then she arranged the materials for reading and science. Finally, she distributed papers which she had corrected over the weekend to the various desks grouped around the room. Again the metallic clatter of the bell cut the stillness to signal the start of a new day in school.

The morning ran smoothly along the plans that Maria had made. Reading was first. Three groups worked at their seats on practice exercises while the fourth group read aloud for Maria. It took over an hour for Maria to hear all of the groups read. She made notes about the oral reading to extend the diagnoses she had made last week. Then it was time to teach the whole class how to define a word with the use of a dictionary. Using ROPES, Maria taught her learners how to perform the skill. Again she used different exercises and materials for the varied reading abilities in the class. Circulating around the classroom, she observed the learners doing the skill. Janet, Patrice, and John were falling far behind in the assigned work. Maria called them over to the large table for extra attention.

She said, "This work seems to be taking a long time."

Looking down at her paper, Janet wiggled her pencil back and forth. John had trouble sitting still, his eyes darting back and forth between Maria and his paper. A sharp intake of breath indicated that Patrice was on the verge of tears.

Maria responded to their feeling and meaning. "You feel bad because the work is hard."

"This work is awful hard, Miss Burbank. I jes' can't find the words," answered Janet.

"She's right! How the heck do you find the right word. They're so many words that start with the same letter," joined in John.

Mutely, Patrice nodded her head in agreement, not trusting her voice.

Janet and John had personalized the meaning themselves so Maria personalized their problem. "You feel bad because you can't find the words quickly in the dictionary."

This time it was Patrice's turn to speak up. "I can't keep up with the others. I guess I don't know how to find the words. Can you help me, Miss Burbank?"

Maria had considered what she had learned about personalizing last year. She knew from her practice teaching that many times the learners would personalize their own deficiencies. They would ask her directly to help them out with what was holding them back. Others would muddle through the learning assignment just as Janet, John, and Patrice were doing. These students need Maria's responding and personalizing skills before they are ready for extra help.

PERSONALIZING THE PROBLEM

A further step in personalizing the meaning is to personalize the problem. You can personalize the problem by shifting the focus to what the learners are unable to do, that is, where they have a behavioral deficit. In doing so, you may modify the format as follows:

"You feel_____ because you cannot_____."

Sometimes, you will find yourself going directly to personalizing the problem. However, do so with care. Personalizing the meaning provides an intermediary step that makes the personalized problem more acceptable to the learners.

You consider the content deficit your learners are experiencing with respect to facts, concepts, principles, skills, and skill steps. You have already learned that responding helps you diagnose that deficit. If you understand that the learners cannot do the skill successfully, you personalize that problem: "You feel sad because you cannot find the answers in the chapter." "You're upset because you can't do this division correctly."

In another situation your learners may not be able to do all the skill steps, so you personalize that problem: "You're confused because you left out the second step." "You feel bad because you can't weigh the sample accurately."

For others, you may diagnose the principle as being the content deficit. When you personalize the problem you say: "You feel angry because you don't understand why the pulley works that way." "You're mixed-up because you don't know the commutative principle of multiplication."

The facts and concepts may be the deficit of other learners. Personalizing this deficit you say: "You're mad because you know how to do the multiplication but you can't remember which reciprocal to use." "You feel dumb because you don't know what 'longitude' is."

Remember that your students can feel good because they can do the skill or skill steps or that they know the supportive knowledge. These good feelings should be acknowledged just as you acknowledge the bad feelings. The chart below illustrates the relationship between feelings and content.

PERSONALIZING THE PROBLEM

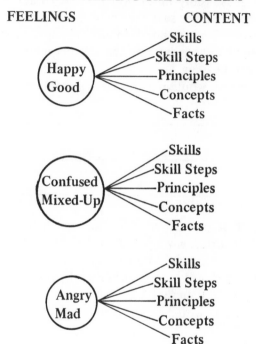

FEELINGS / CONTENT

Happy Good — Skills, Skill Steps, Principles, Concepts, Facts

Confused Mixed-Up — Skills, Skill Steps, Principles, Concepts, Facts

Angry Mad — Skills, Skill Steps, Principles, Concepts, Facts

Practicing Personalizing the Learners' Problems

Personalizing your learners' problems will take some practice. Below are some examples of student expressions. They are ready for your personalized response to the problem. Do not forget to include a feeling word.

Student A is visibly upset over his lack of ability with a pair of scissors. He has said that he doesn't want to use the 'dumb' scissors. You respond to his feeling and meaning. While noting that he is holding the scissors incorrectly, you personalize his meaning.

Write how you would personalize his problem.

_____

_____

_____

Student B is puzzled over her answer in multiplication which she has gotten wrong. At first she blames the book for having the wrong answer. You respond and personalize the feeling and meaning. Looking at her work, you diagnose that her problem is thinking that $7 \times 6 = 44$.

Write how you would personalize her problem.

_____

_____

_____

Student C is elated that he did so well on the English exam. "I don't know how I did so good. I thought I had the wrong definitions on the vocabulary list," he says. You personalize his feeling and meaning. You remember that he did so well because he spelled the words correctly as well as writing the correct definitions.

Write how you would personalize his problem.

PERSONALIZING THE FEELING

Trooping in the door after morning recess, Maria's class settled down into their seats. "What's next, Miss Burbank," called out John from the back of the room. Others joined in.

"I hope it's something new."

"Yeah, how about somethin' different, Miss Burbank?"

Maria smiled, "You've never been a weatherperson have you?"

"You mean like Tom Frost on Channel 2?"

"That's right," answered Maria. "Last week we talked about the temperature and how it affects the weather. Today we're going to use some of the equipment Mr. Frost uses to predict the weather."

Maria divided up the class and assigned them to the five different lab stations she had set up around the room. She circulated among the groups making sure everyone understood the directions. Noticing an unusual amount of noise from Tony's group, she made her way to that corner of the room. It seemed that the other four members of the group had formed a coalition against Tony's leadership.

"What seems to be the trouble here?" questioned Maria.

"Tony won't let us do anything," responded Janet.

"Yeah, he hogs the whole thing," joined in Theresa.

"He thinks he knows it all," added Kenneth. Michael nodded his assent.

Maria responded to their content, "You're saying that Tony won't give you a chance to do a part of the experiment."

Noting their agreement with her response, she continued, "You feel pretty angry." Again they nodded their heads.

Next she responded to their feeling and meaning. "You feel angry because Tony won't let you in on the learning."

As the four students voiced their agreement, Maria knew that she had to personalize their meaning. Otherwise they would continue to focus on Tony and not what they could do to change the situation to their advantage. "You feel angry because you want a chance to learn how to use the centigrade thermometer."

"But how are we gonna get a chance with Tony?" asked Theresa with discouragement.

Maria turned to face Theresa, "You feel upset because you don't know how to get Tony to let you use the thermometer."

Not only had Maria personalized the problem for Theresa but she also personalized her feelings.

Theresa and the other children did not feel angry with themselves. Their feelings of anger were directed towards Tony. When Maria personalized their problem, their feelings were now more of confusion as to how to deal with Tony. It would not be appropriate to continue to use "angry" as the feeling word. That is why Maria changed the feeling word to "upset."

Evaluating the Learners' Feelings[10]

You personalize the meaning by considering the implications of the experience for the learners' behavior. Now you will further personalize the feeling. You personalize the feeling by considering the implications for the learners' feelings of the personalized meaning response.

Personalizing the feeling and the meaning provides you with a means for going beyond what the learners have expressed. The techniques of personalizing allow you to search out new, deeper, and more accurate feelings and meanings in responding to the learners.

Personalizing Responses

Now let us examine more translations to the classroom situation. Begin to respond to the more personal feeling and meaning expressed by the learners with whom you have been able to respond accurately at the feeling and meaning level. Perhaps Andy has come to you to complain about the treatment another teacher has been giving him. And perhaps you've laid an effective base for personalizing by responding to his explicit feeling and meaning six or more times — responses along the lines of, "You feel furious because Mr. Smith seems to pick on you unfairly." Now you might begin to respond at a more personalized level by saying "You feel furious because you're the only person he treats like that." This response personalizes the meaning which the situation has for Andy. You might then go on to personalize the problem in terms of a behavioral deficit and the new feeling (if any) which Andy's perception of this deficit may arouse.

Try this with at least one learner a day. Extend the number of *"You feel_____because you (cannot) _____"* responses you make in a row. If you can make six personalized responses with the feeling and meaning to each learner, then you are ready to learn additive skills. Remember, if the learners continue to explore new material, your responses have been interchangeable.

---

[10]For more information on personalizing feelings see the References section.

Practicing Personalizing the Learners' Feeling

Examine the following classroom excerpts and decide which of them need a new feeling word for the personalized response. Then write a response that would personalize the feeling and the problem.

Teacher's Response to Feeling and Meaning:

"You feel great because the class gave you the most votes."

Personalized Problem: You aren't sure you can do a good job as President.

Personalize the Feeling and Problem: _____

_____

_____

Teacher's Response to Feeling and Meaning:

"You feel mad because I made the test so hard."

Personalized Problem: You didn't know the facts and concepts of map-reading.

Personalize the Feeling and Problem: _____

_____

_____

Teacher's Response to Feeling and Meaning:

"You feel mixed-up about what to do next in the division problem."

Personalized Problem: You don't know where to put the first digit of the answer.

Personalize the Feeling and Problem: _____

Using Maria's Experience

As you have noted, Maria is doing several things simultaneously as she personalizes. First, she is helping her learners understand the strengths and deficits of their content. When you personalize for your own learners, you will help them understand what they know and what they do not know. The diagnosis that you make while you respond will enhance the accuracy of your personalized response to the learners. You have also seen that you may have to change the feeling word when you personalize. That is because your learners are moving from exploring their problems with you to understanding them. Eventually, you will help your learners to manage their own learning. They will be able to personalize their own learning deficits so that they will say:

"We're really mixed-up because we don't know how to do this third step."

STATING THE GOALS

"I can't find the answer, Miss Burbank." Michael's freckled nose wrinkled with digust. Aimlessly he turned the pages of his Social Studies text to emphasize the hopelessness of the assignment.

"Which question is giving you such a hard time, Michael?"

"All of them!" he replied, holding his head in his hand. "I haven't found one answer!"

"You feel bad because you can't even begin the assignment, Michael."

"Well, I won't ever get it finished in time." He shook his head slowly, back and forth.

"You feel bad because you won't be able to finish the assignment if you can't find the answers. You want to be able to find the answers to the questions."

Michael looked perplexed. "But **how** do you find the answers. That's what I need to know."

What Maria has done is to help Michael understand what his learning goal is. She knows that he wants to complete the assignment. Then she has to determine what skill, skill steps, or supportive knowledge is Michael's learning goal.

Adding to the Learners' Understanding[11]

Responsive skills have facilitated the learners' exploration of where they are in relation to themselves, to you, and to the learning material. Now we are going to make personalized understanding responses in the context of a responsive base. Where the learners want to be is understood most easily in terms of their personalized problems: the goal is the flip-side of the problem. You can understand where they want to be if you understand what deficits limit them to where they are. The goal here is for you to establish a direction which the learners can use within their frames of reference. You can do this by responding to the discrepancy between where the learners are and where they want to be, or need to be. The longer you explore the learners' concerns, the easier these steps will be.

First, think about where the learners are saying they are in their past few responses.

Second, think about any behaviors or capabilities that the learners lack.

Third, think about where the learners are saying they are in relation to where they want to be.

Fourth, think about what feeling they have about that goal.

Fifth, formulate a response as follows: *"You feel _____ because you (cannot)_____ and you want to_____."*

While feeling continues to be important in these responses, personalized understanding usually emphasizes the meaning. It is the meaning which gives the direction and guidance to the learners. For example, here is a boy speaking to his teacher:

Learner: *"I didn't make the team."*

Teacher: *"You feel really discouraged because you didn't measure up and you want very much to measure up."*

The teacher responds to the boy's initial discouragement and the reason for it. This is where the student is. The teacher then supplies a direction by personalizing his understanding of the implied goal of catching up. All this is done from within the learner's frame of reference. Here is an illustration involving another young student:

Teacher: *"You feel pretty disappointed because you just haven't been able to handle math and you want to be a business person and this requires a good math background."*

Again, the teacher has responded to the learner's disappointment and the reason for this disappointment. But she has also personalized her response to the goal implied by the learner's expression. Here is a last example, an elementary school girl to the teacher:

Learner: *"Those kids keep calling me 'fatso' because I'm so big. Well, if they don't cut it out, they're gonna find out how big I am!"*

Teacher: *"You're angry with them and with yourself, too, because you let them make fun of your size and you want to stop them from treating you that way."*

Again, the teacher responds to where the learner is and where she wants to go.

---

[11]For more information on personalizing problems and goals, see References section.

Personalizing Understanding in the Classroom

Let us make some translations toward responding with direction to learners in the classroom. Again, first pick the learners with whom you have been able to respond successfully in the past. You can respond to them again using both the *"You feel_____because_____"* and the *"You feel_____because you (cannot)_____"* format. This will give you the responsive base that you need. Now formulate a response that captures both where the learners are and where they want to be. Utilize the following format in doing so, *"You feel_____because you (cannot)_____and you want to_____."* Remember poor picked-upon Andy a few pages back. You might eventually respond to him by saying, "You feel miserable because you can't figure out how to get on Mr. Smith's good side and you really want him to act friendly toward you." When you know that you can make personalized responses to your learners with some facility, then you are ready to get a further understanding of the exercises that you have completed.

You can personalize understanding for a large group of learners in the classroom. This might involve simply flipping over the personalized group problem to determine the personalized group goal. For example, if you have personalized the group problem ("cannot do") you may personalize the group goal ("can do").

Personalizing Fully in the Classroom

When you put your personalized responses to feeling, meaning, problems, and goals together, you personalize fully in the classroom. This means identifying the feelings, the goals, and the benefits to be accomplished.

You may personalize the group goal ("can do") by attacking the benefits in terms of the personalized group feeling ("good") and meaning ("getting it right"). This will enable you to define the goal and the benefits to be achieved.

You can make several applications of personalizing in the classroom. Again, include the interactions between learners as well as between you and the learners. For example, you might personalize the understanding of a small group of learners who are unable to perform a particular skill but really want to be able to do so: *"You all feel bad because you can't figure out this material and you really want to get the assignment right."* Try to make sure that you personalize fully with each learner before the beginning of each new unit of learning. That way, you will always be able to relate the learners' frames of reference to the learning goals. Later on, you may want to teach your learners directly how to personalize their own understanding in learning.

PERSONALIZING PROBLEMS AND GOALS

In many cases, the learners' goals will be one level removed from their problem. Think back to those learners whose problem was finding the vocabulary words in the dictionary. They will need the skill steps necessary to perform that skill. In other words, if the problem is a skill deficit then the goal will be to learn the skill steps of the skill deficit.

PERSONALIZED PROBLEM: **PERSONALIZED GOAL:**

SKILL #1

SKILL #1 ————————————▶ SKILL STEPS

When the learners are having a problem implementing the skill steps, their goal will be to learn the supportive knowledge they are missing. If the learners' problem is that they cannot understand why the skill steps work that way, then their goal is to learn the necessary principles of the skill. Kenneth could not perform the subtraction skill steps correctly because he did not understand the concepts of regrouping. His problem was the skill steps, his goal will be to learn the necessary concepts. Another example of the acquisition of supportive knowledge as the goal is the girl who could not get the right multiplication answer. Her problem was performing the skill steps correctly, her goal was to learn the fact, 7 x 6 = 42.

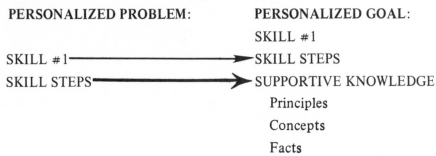

PERSONALIZED PROBLEM: **PERSONALIZED GOAL:**

SKILL #1

SKILL #1 ————————————➤ SKILL STEPS

SKILL STEPS ————————————➤ SUPPORTIVE KNOWLEDGE

       Principles

       Concepts

       Facts

If the supportive knowledge is the problem, then your learner's goal may be to learn a new skill. For the learner who did not know the map-reading facts and concepts, the goal could be the skill of keeping a notebook of definitions, or the skills of studying for a test.

PERSONALIZED PROBLEM: PERSONALIZED GOAL:

SKILL #1

SKILL #1 ——————————→ SKILL STEPS

SKILL STEPS ——————————→ SUPPORTIVE KNOWLEDGE

    Principles

    Concepts

    Facts

SUPPORTIVE KNOWLEDGE ——→ SKILL #2

    Principles

    Concepts

    Facts

Laying a responsive base allows you to diagnose most accurately the problem of your learners. Knowing your content allows you to help the learners set appropriate learning goals to remedy the problem.

Practicing Setting Goals for the Learners

As a final exercise of personalizing, take the excerpts which you used to personalize the problem and personalize the feelings. Add the goal statement you would give each of these learners. These excerpts appear in this chapter. Additionally, you could practice your personalizing and responding skills with your friends and students.

Write a response to personalize the feeling, problem, and goals:

1. Student A, whose problem was a lack of scissor skills.

_____

_____

2. Student B, whose problem is completing the multiplication examples correctly.

_____

_____

3. Student C, who spelled the vocabulary words correctly.

_____

_____

4. The student who is unsure that he can do a good job as president.

_____

_____

5. The student who does not know the facts and concepts of map-reading.

_____

_____

6. The student who does not know all the steps of division.

_____

_____

Monday

Today was an "okay" day. The kids are mostly great! They really are beginning to trust me. And I'm learning more about them each day.

I feel pretty good about how my lesson plans are working out, although sometimes the class resembles a 3-ring circus. I have to work on keeping things simple for these kids.

I've learned that they want to do a good job in school. But some of them have had too many bad experiences. So when I give them something too hard, they begin to act out. John can't sit still when he's frustrated and manages to keep everyone around him from their work. Kenneth swears like a sailor when he can't succeed, while Janet shuts down all systems and goes off to the moon.

There really is a lot more to teaching than giving assignments and correcting papers. It's giving the right assignment. To do that I've got to respond to the kids to make sure I understand what they know and what they don't know. It's important for me to personalize what they need to know. Then I have to figure out a plan right away. I think that's the hardest part of my day.

Using Maria's Experience

You will use personalizing skills to help the learners understand their problem and what can be done about it. But there is another side to personalizing: presentation. Each learning goal that you set for your learners must be accompanied by a curriculum which includes your content and methods. In many cases, the content will need to be developed on the spot. Tom may need the steps of using a ruler. Julie may need a program to learn the missing facts of the skill steps. Jessica may need some help in planning her assignments so that she can finish her work on time. These students cannot wait until tomorrow. They need this help right now. Each one of your learners, at one time or another, will have a unique need that you will have to fulfill. While you may be able to develop your content spontaneously, planning the **tell, show, do** methods of ROPES may present a more difficult problem. You personalize the teaching delivery by selecting **tell** methods that this particular learner can use most efficiently. The **show** method must come from the learner's frame of reference. Most critically, you must select a **do** method with which the learner can succeed. For it is your learners' success with learning that measures your success with teaching.

The late afternoon sun warmed the air in Maria's classroom. It intensified the smell of children which hung in the still air. That puppy-like-smell mixed with chalk dust was not unpleasant. Rather it was part of the setting, a reminder of those who lived in the room for most of the day. As she corrected her learners' assignments, Maria was startled by a noise at the door. Looking up she saw Kenneth peering in at her.

"Hello, Kenneth! How was your game?"

"Aw, the other kids had to go home."

"Can I do something for you?"

Kenneth edged into the classroom, keeping his eyes on the floor, "Uh. . .uh. . . I wondered, . . .um. . .um. . . Can I help ya," he suddenly shot out.

Maria put her papers to one side. "How about helping me set up tomorrow's experiment for science?"

Kenneth nodded his head vigorously, looking up at Maria. His eyes shone for an instant, then he looked guarded once more. He dropped his eyes to the floor.

"Okay," he mumbled. "I guess I can do that."

Maria began to give directions, as she thought with much emotion, "Oh, Kenneth. How can I help you. . .really help you learn to live?"

Reinforcing the Learners 5

USING NEGATIVE REINFORCEMENT

The leaden sky opened with a rush of rain, splattering down on the city. Sheets of water ran down the tall windows of Maria's classroom. The children stared vacantly at the rain, drugged by the sound and the humidity of the storm. Maria had to consciously pull herself out of her stupor and refocus her attention on her teaching.

"These kids need some excitement," she thought, "or else they're all going to fall asleep." Mentally reviewing her plans, she decided that her math leasson would never be able to compete with the storm outside.

"I've got to come up with a smash . . . something they can all get involved in doing . . . something that they really like to do."

Quickly she examined her options, deciding to start this rainy morning off with the social studies project she had planned for later in the week. Luckily, most of the materials she needed were available. However, they were not organized.

Clapping her hands together, Maria drew the learners' attention away from the storm. "Today we are going to make dioramas."

The children began to look interested. Like a giant awakening, twenty-five students began to stretch and move, growing taller in their seats, reacting to the enthusiasm in Maria's voice.

"Hey, good!" "I hope it's fun!" "What's a diorama?"

"Remember the shoeboxes I asked you to bring to school?" Maria indicated a pile of boxes stacked at the back of the room. "Those are going to be windows. Windows that you can look into and see what happened in the United States a long time ago."

Manny looked disbelievingly at Julie sitting next to him. Julie snickered at his gesture that indicated Maria must have some screws loose.

Maria smiled at Manny, understanding his disbelief. "You're saying that you don't think it's possible for an old shoebox to become a window, Manny."

Manny grinned back sheepishly, shaking his head.

"Have you ever built a model, Manny?"

"Yeah, I put together an airplane this summer."

"Well, today you will help build a history model inside a shoebox."

The learners looked around at one another with mixed emotions, some with disbelief, others with trepidation, and still others with anticipation.

Maria moved quickly around the room, scooping up the necessary materials for the dioramas. Dividing the students into groups of two, she assigned different scenes to each group. She spread an assortment of pipe-cleaners, pebbles, cotton, string, clothespins, and clay on a table in the center of the room. On another, she put out a rainbow of construction paper, paints, crayons, scissors, and paste. The room began to hum with activity as pairs of learners collected their necessary materials. Maria supervised with a feeling of satisfaction. By her initiative she had pulled her students out of the doldrums and into learning.

Her feelings of satisfaction were short-lived, however. In the back of the room, Julie and Janet were hilariously enjoying a battle with bits of clay, a snowball fight in miniature. Maria grimaced to herself. Should she ignore the high spirits or confront their inappropriate behavior? Perhaps she should respond to them so that they would understand the implications of their disruptive behavior. These thoughts quickly flashed through Maria's mind as she made her way over to Julie and Janet.

"Stop that this minute, Julie! Pick that clay up immediately, both of you. Since you can't work with these materials properly, you will have to go back to your desks and write individual reports."

The girls looked up at Maria with amazement. Her tone of voice froze them for an instant. They heard the edge of Maria's voice. Then they dived under their table, picking up bits of clay littering the floor around them, eyes down with embarrassment. Other learners smirked knowingly at one another, relieved that they had not drawn Maria's disapproval.

Maria had made her decision to negatively reinforce the disruptive behavior of Janet and Julie. If she had ignored their behavior, it would indicate her disinterest in how they were engaging in the learning task. Because Maria wanted her learners to work constructively, she found that she could not ignore how the two girls chose to use their time. Also, the situation did not warrant the attention Maria would need to give in order to respond to their behavior. That would detract from the learning time of the other twenty-three students in the class. Instead, Maria dispatched her reinforcement quickly so that the class could continue with their learning tasks.

Examining Negative Reinforcement

The use of reinforcements is so simple, you are often not aware you are using them. Reinforcements are everywhere. They exist in the eye contact you make with the learners, your posture, involuntary gestures, or facial expressions with which you react to the learners' behavior. Even when you correct an assignment, you are reinforcing the learners' behavior with a mark of X or C, or a grade of A to F.

Negative reinforcement is required in certain situations. If the learners' behavior is negative, you will reinforce negatively. During the action phase of learning, when all behavior can be ultimately classified as moving in the direction of the skill goal or not, negative reinforcement is essential. The students must know what they are doing, right or wrong, in order to become proficient in the skill.

Following the Steps of Negative Reinforcement

More specifically, the reinforcement should first indicate your evaluation or reaction to the behavior. You should express your judgment of behaviors that move your learners away from their goals: *"These examples are wrong,"* or *"This is not the time to talk."*

Next you should give your learners the reason why they have earned your judgment: *"These examples are wrong because you didn't reduce the fraction,"* or *"This is not the time to talk because you won't be able to finish your work."*

Finally, you should give a prescription to remedy the problem. You will want the learners to go back and relearn the skills that are keeping them from obtaining their goals: *"These examples are wrong because you didn't reduce the fractions. Go back to page 46 and practice these examples using common factors."* Or *"This is not the time to talk because you won't be able to finish your work. Work at this desk by yourself away from the other students."*

When you use negative reinforcement you may find it easier to use this format: *"That's (teacher's evaluation) because (reason) . Now, you should (prescription) ."*

Reinforcement Discriminations

There are certain discriminations that Maria makes when she uses negative reinforcement. The first is the intensity of her behavior or the strength of her reaction. She evaluates how serious the learner's behavior really is and matches her reinforcement to that behavior. A minor indiscretion receives a minor negative reinforcement. This may take the form of a mild confrontation about the discrepancy between how the students are behaving and how they express themselves as behaving. Perhaps the students' view of what is happening does not match what Maria sees. Then she would confront the discrepancy by saying, *"You've told me you are doing your work but you have only done one question."* If the learners' behaviors are more negative, to the point of endangering themselves or others, Maria will react with strong negative reinforcement.

Another discrimination that Maria must make when using negative reinforcement is to use her diagnosis of the learners to select an appropriate negative reinforcement. For some students, a look or a step toward them will be enough to negatively reinforce a minor negative behavior. Maria may have to speak firmly with others and even use punishments for a few. With reinforcement there is no such thing as equal treatment. In order to be effective, it must be appropriate for each learner's frame of reference.

Several learner incidents are described below. They include some information about the learners involved in the negative behavior. Practice using your discriminations and write down what you would say or do if you were the teacher in each situation.

Student A is physically aggressive during recess. She has few friends because of her bullying behavior. You have taken time to talk with her about the problem several times. Today, you observe her hitting, pushing, and shoving others to get to the front of the line on the playground. What would you do? What would you say?

_____

_____

_____

_____

Student B who is usually a model student has not completed an assignment although he had plenty of time to do so. What would you do? What would you say?

_____

_____

_____

_____

140

You have just confiscated an obscene note from Student
C with specific reference to you. Student C has not been a
problem before in class. In fact, you are rather surprised
because this student generally wants your approval. What
would you do? What would you say?

_____

_____

_____

_____

There is an inherent danger in using negative reinforcement in the classroom. That is why so many teachers are reluctant to use it. You want the focus on your teaching to be a positive one. Most importantly, you have seen too many teachers who are predominantly negative reinforcers. These are the screamers and the grouches you have all met at one time or another. But ignoring your learners' negative behavior is not going to help them grow. You know that. And just as Maria has done, you will on occasion use negative reinforcement. Then your learners will learn that they are not moving toward the learning goal. You may want to think of yourself as the navigator, who, finding the ship off course, takes initiative to move in the charted direction, not because it is easy, but because it is your job.

Tuesday

What a miserable day it was today. . .in more ways than one. It poured buckets of rain and the teaching wasn't that great either. But I learned. . .the hard way. . .that changing plans isn't always a good idea. I thought the kids needed some excitement. . .well, they got it. If I never see another shoebox again, I'll be happy! I just hadn't planned all the details and my kids had never made 3-dimensional models before. That should have been my daily skill and I should have broken that skill down into steps. Instead, I spent most of my time saying. . . "Don't do that!" "Put that down!" "Get busy!" Yes, it was really my fault that the kids got out of hand. I hadn't spent enough time planning.

Using Maria's Experience

You should examine your teaching behavior if your learners are excessively negative in their learning behavior. Maria found that her spontaneous action brought about negative behavior in her learners. They seemed to sense that her learning goal was not clearly defined. They did not have the skills to do what she was asking them to do. There are other examples of teaching which may produce negative behaviors in the learners. You may be spending too much time with a few learners. The others will know that your attention is not focused on them and they act accordingly. Your teaching may lack variety and your learners' boredom may direct them away from the learning goal. In other instances, the learning goals you set for the learners may not be congruent with what your learners perceive to be important. Use your learners' responses to diagnose your teaching.

USING NEUTRAL REINFORCEMENT

"Hey, Miss Burbank," Tony called out from his math group. "It's time for lunch!"

"Sure enough, Tony! We almost missed it," Maria said with a smile. "Put your games away until after lunch, class."

Immediately the sounds of the classroom changed key. There was the rustle of brown paper bags. Some children had to stand to search their pockets for lunch money. Others rummaged inside their desks. Finding what was needed, they moved to the edge of their seats, awaiting the countdown to line up.

"I forgot my lunch money, Miss Burbank," said Patrice in a small voice. Maria reached into her purse and drew out thirty-five cents.

"Bring it in tomorrow, Patrice."

Maria walked over to the doorway. She had to smile at the change that the thought of food brought about in her students. They all focused on her expectantly. After Maria nodded her head to signal them, the students lined up with just enough restraint to prevent being sent back to their seats.

The sounds and smells of the cafeteria rushed to meet Maria's class as they approached the room. Sniffing the air, Maria determined that it was Pizza Day at Washington School. Once inside, some students disappeared into lines, while others found seats at empty tables.

Maria found the lunchroom monitor and said, "It's my first day on lunchroom duty. Maybe you can fill me in on what I'm supposed to do."

"Sure can, Miss Burbank. You're a new teacher here this year? I'm Jim Johnson." While he talked to Maria he never took his eyes off the children around the room. "The main thing is to watch the kids so that they don't throw food around or fight." Jim began moving toward one of the lines where there was some minor shoving. Maria followed to catch the words of wisdom from this veteran lunchroom monitor.

The children in the line saw Jim coming and, knowing the consequences of shoving, ceased their pushing. The crash of a tray sent Jim off in a new direction. "Now that's all right, honey," he consoled. "We'll just get you another tray." Jim sent the girl off to a line and efficiently scooped up the scramble of pizza and peaches on the floor.

"Get the idea, Miss Burbank? You take this side. I'll be over here if you need me."

Maria looked around at the tables full of children giggling, talking, and eating. This was certainly different from the classroom. "Look at that kid. His lunch is three ice cream sandwiches and two bottles of milk!" She shook her head and walked by the table without a word. By the trash barrel stood another student emptying an untouched dinner into the garbage. "Look at that waste," she said to herself. "These kids' eating habits are abominable."

"How's your lunch, John?" She questioned a familiar face. John was happily stuffing a sandwich into his mouth. "What have you got today?"

"Ketchup," he answered.

"A ketchup sandwich?" repeated Maria carefully.

"Yeah," said John. "My favorite kind!"

Again she showed no response. Instead she walked to the next table quickly. "Ketchup sandwiches! I don't believe it. These kids just don't know what they're supposed to eat!"

Maria couldn't bring herself to react openly to the student's eating habits. She knew so little about the students on her first day of cafeteria duty, she decided to find out what she could before mounting a nutrition crusade.

Giving Neutral Reinforcement

Simply stated, if it is not positive and it is not negative, it is neutral. How do you give neutral reinforcement? That is precisely the point. You do not. You simply do not respond to the behavior. The students do something and get no response from you.

Neutral reinforcements provide you with another option. Instead of having to respond to everything, you may choose not to respond to some things. The neutral response is predominantly used by ineffective teachers. They may rationalize neutral reinforcements with theories and philosophies ranging from "democratic idealism" through "do your own thing." What it means, basically, is that the teacher ignores the students.

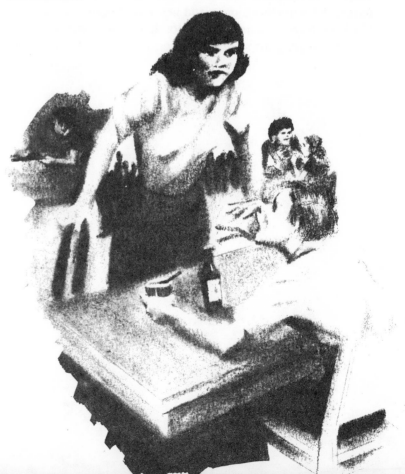

Suspending Your Judgment

For effective teachers, the neutral response is really a suspended judgment. It dictates an active observation rather than a passive neglect of student behavior. It dictates vigilance rather than vagrancy in the classroom. You may even say, "I'll watch you to see how well you do this."

The vigilance is instrumental. If a particular behavior is moving the learners closer to the goal, then you positively reinforce it. If it moves them away from the goal, then you negatively reinforce it. You respond neutrally only when you are not sure which direction the students are moving in. Usually, you respond neutrally because you do not have your teaching and learning programs together to a point where you can determine the direction of a particular behavior. Sometimes you respond neutrally because the student has introduced a behavior that you have not observed before. At best, then, neutral reinforcements are stop-gap measures.

Neutral Reinforcement is Really Vigilance

Let us examine Maria's lunchroom reactions with respect to neutral reinforcement. She was in a new situation. Many of the students were not in her class. The result was that she did not have enough information to react to the students' behavior. "Why should John be eating ketchup sandwiches?" Perhaps there was nothing else at home with which to make lunches. Perhaps John made his own lunch. Maria would need more information about John before she would initiate negative reinforcement.

The other two students were not Maria's. She would not be assigned lunchroom duty for another three weeks. Even if she did admonish the ice cream eater and the tray dumper, they would continue to eat ice cream and throw away food when other monitors were on duty. Lacking information and the ability to follow through, Maria's neutral reinforcement was really vigilance with respect to the students' nutritional behavior.

Practicing Neutral Reinforcement

Think back to your experience in the classroom as a student, observer, or teacher. Describe one situation where neutral reinforcement was used appropriately. Then describe another situation where it was used inappropriately.

Appropriate Neutral Reinforcement: _____

_____

_____

_____

_____

_____

_____

Inappropriate Neutral Reinforcement: _____

_____

_____

_____

_____

_____

_____

Wednesday

After school, I went and had a talk with Lois Morse, the counselor, about John's ketchup sandwich. She reminded me that he is a state ward in a foster home. That means that he is eligible for a lunch pass. We decided that he probably made his own lunch today and really does like ketchup sandwiches. She promised to follow up with a visit to the lunch-room tomorrow to check up on him. Then we talked about the nutritional habits of the other students. We decided that the whole staff would have to get behind the effort. Lois suggested that I talk to Bob Abbott about that.

I think what those kids eat is important enough to get upset about. . . to want to do something about. Those kids go home and live on pop and potato chips. While they're with us, we should be able to teach them how to eat. It isn't enough to teach them reading and math. We have to teach them how to live a healthy life! I'll see Bob Abbott tomorrow.

Using Maria's Experience

There were two instances when Maria used neutral reinforcement. The first was when there was no established goal for the students' eating habits. There will be many times when you will use neutral reinforcement because you have not set a goal. You have no measure of the students' behavior. It may not seem relevant to you whether or not your students chew gum. Therefore, you will ignore that behavior because it does not relate to any of your goals. But once you have established with your learners that you do not want them to chew gum, you will reinforce positively and negatively with respect to that goal.

Another instance where Maria used neutral reinforcement was when she was gathering information. She tried to find out just why John would be eating ketchup sandwiches before she reacted negatively to his choice. Likewise, you may have set a goal with your students that you expect them to respect each other. When you observe their interactions, you will use positive and negative reinforcements, depending upon the behavior. You will use neutral reinforcement only when you cannot determine the nature of the student's actions.

USING POSITIVE REINFORCEMENT

"Hey, Angela," yelled Janet. "Wait for us, Patrice and Theresa are coming too." Janet stood in the doorway of Maria's classroom. The last bell had rung, the buses had all been dispatched. Turning toward Maria she said, "We're gonna go get a shake, Miss Burbank, 'cause we're celebratin' Theresa's new baby brother. I'm gonna treat her." Janet fought her way into her sweater.

"That's great, Janet. I like the way you girls are thoughtful of each other. You will always have **good** friends, Janet," complimented Maria.

"Yeah, I guess I will," reflected Janet. "Well, see 'ya tomorrow. C'mon Patrice, Theresa . . . Let's go!"

Maria had to smile at their enthusiasm as she watched the four girls run down the corridor to the stairs, then out into the brilliant autumn sunshine.

Shuffling through the dried leaves on the sidewalk, the girls chattered on about school that day.

"School sure is fun this year," sighed Theresa. "Everything good is happening to me, a new teacher . . . and now a new brother."

"Yeah, Miss Burbank is real nice. She makes me feel good about school," agreed Janet. "Not like Mrs. Snow!"

The girls all groaned in unison. "What a pain she was," added Patrice. "Don't do that! Stop it! That's wrong," she mimicked with her voice as well as with gestures their last year's teacher.

This sent all the girls off into gales of laughter. "My poor brother has her this year," said Patrice. "But he's pretty good at driving teachers crazy."

"Well, Miss Burbank is different," said Angela emphatically.

"C'mon, let's get there today!" Theresa set off at a fast sprint, her long legs striding ahead of the others. They followed, trying without success to catch her.

The four girls settled down around a table to enjoy their cool thick shakes.

"Hey, how did you guys do on that story we had to write. You know . . . the settings we had to describe?" This was an assignment which Maria had given, culminating five days of language arts lessons. Janet's question, although seemingly nonchalant, was asked with much control. Inside, she was happy as could be with what Miss Burbank had written on her assignment. But she could not show her friends how excited she really was over the good grade. That would be too much like . . . bragging!

Angela smiled and spoke first. "Miss Burbank really liked what I wrote. She says she's gonna give me another soccer lesson 'cause I did such a good job."

"I guess she liked mine, too," said Patrice proudly. "She put mine up on the board!"

"Mine, too," exclaimed Theresa.

Janet smiled with satisfaction. Her friends had done a good job, too. But she had gotten the best reward of all! "Miss Burbank is gonna have me be the office messenger all next week because I did such a good job. I never got a chance ever . . . before. The other teacher always picked your brains to go. Miss Burbank picked me!"

Providing Verbal Positive Reinforcement

Just as you give nourishment and unconditional regard to a young child starting out in life, so you give positive regard to a student just starting out in learning. The students begin to learn a skill by exploring the parts. They analyze the steps. Their inquiry leads to the discovery of relationships. They go on to understand. They need your encouragement. You give them positive reinforcement. Providing positive reinforcement means you want **them** to feel good about what they have done. You want them to know **you** feel good about what they have done.

The easiest way to give positive feedback is orally. You respond positively to the students when they give a correct answer, volunteer information, or initiate some desirable action. "That's good, Pat! You mean if you were certain that was the problem, you could rewind the motor."

Providing Written Positive Reinforcement

The next most frequent form of positive reinforcement is in writing. This refers to what you write on the students' classwork, homework, tests, and quizzes. There are only two criteria you can respond to: quality and quantity. You may want to make two positive comments on major papers, one for quality and one for quantity of performance. On daily papers you will only be reinforcing the skill of the day, be it quality or quantity. In either case, you will need to explain to the students the criteria you will use to judge their effectiveness. You may also choose to develop these standards with the class.

Other rewards may take the form of recognition, if appropriate. You may use some learners' work as a model for other learners. The displays and exhibits around the classroom offer you this opportunity. On some occasions you may want to take the learners' work out into the community if a special reward is appropriate.

Using the Steps of Positive Reinforcement

You will include three dimensions when you use positive reinforcement. First you will indicate your approval. Then you will tell the students how their behavior is moving them toward their goal. Finally, you will reward that behavior with a chance to learn new skills which may or may not be related to the accomplishment of the goal.

Using the same format used for negative reinforcement, you will say: *"That's good work, John, because you punctuated all these sentences correctly. Now you can finish the Social Studies project you started this morning."* Simply stated, the format is: *"That's (teacher's evaluation) because (reason) . Now you can (reward) ."*

The Three Keys to Positive Reinforcement

There are several aspects to the positive reinforcement that Maria used. First, examine what she said to Janet:

"I like the way you girls are thoughtful to each other. You will always have **good** friends, Janet." Maria has let Janet know verbally that she approves of Janet's behavior which is moving toward the goal of being a good friend. It is important that Maria reinforce the behavior by telling Janet what the goal is.

Another aspect of positive reinforcement is the personalizing of the rewards to the girls. Think back to the kinds of rewards Maria meted out to the four girls for their writing assignments. Angela earned another soccer lesson. Patrice and Theresa earned recognition via the bulletin board, and Janet earned the right to be the office messenger for the week. Marie has given each girl a personalized reward, a reward that means something special to each one.

The third aspect of positive reinforcement is the strength or potency of the reinforcement. If her students had achieved a large goal, Maria would strongly reinforce those behaviors. This was the case with the Language Arts assignment. It was the culmination of five days' learning. For those students who earned Maria's positive reinforcement, she made it very special. On a day-to-day basis, Maria would use positive reinforcement less dramatically, but still personalized for the learners.

Practicing Using Positive Reinforcement

Using the following examples of student behavior, practice giving positive reinforcement. Write down what you would say to the student or write on the assignment. Remember to consider the behavior as it relates to the goal, since the strength of the reinforcement is dependent upon the relationship. Remember to personalize the reward. The format you will use is: *"That's (teacher's evaluation) because (reason) . Now you can (reward) ."*

Gail, who loves to read, has had considerable difficulty understanding the multiplication skills of the past week. She has worked very diligently however, even staying for extra help after school. On the unit test, she gets 80% correct. How would you positively reinforce her behavior?

_____

_____

_____

_____

Tom, a good student and athlete, picks out a book from classic literature to use for a book report. Most students select their books by the least number of pages they can find. How would you positively reinforce his behavior?

_____

_____

_____

152   Abby's behavior is usually very disruptive to those around her. She is continually poking and talking to them. Today, you have not had to speak to her once about her disruptive behavior. You know that one of the reasons she engages in disruptive behavior is to be the center of attention. How would you positively reinforce her behavior?

_____

_____

_____

I was so pleased with the way the kids performed on the language arts assignment. After five days, they had learned how to do something! It's great for a teacher when the kids come through. . .like you really are a teacher. The kids were pretty happy, too.

One thing I've got to remember to do is to praise the kids more often when they do things right. Sometimes I just take their good behavior for granted. Like. . .I expect Tony to help set a good example with his work habits. So today I said, "Tony, you show the others how to work. Your study habits are excellent!" Well, he was just as pleased as could be. Then he set to work with twice as much concentration as before.

Using Maria's Experience

There are several judgments that you will have to make about using positive reinforcement when you teach. If you are already a teacher, have you ever considered if you use enough positive reinforcement when you teach? You may assume that your learners know when you are happy with them. They certainly know when you are not! But yet, the saying, "no news is good news" should not apply to the learners in your classroom. When they are on track, you should tell them in a way that says their behavior is moving toward a goal. It is not enough to smile and say, *"Good."* That is merely an indication of approval, but not of what you approve. Your learners won't know that they had the right answer when you say, *"Next?".* A check on an assignment means only that the assignment was completed. It measures neither the quantity nor the quality.

If you have already taught, have you ever personalized the reinforcement you have given your learners? Not all of them get turned on by gold stars. Many of your learners cannot achieve "A" or "100" on tests. Find out what is important to your learners by using your responding skills. Some may want a baseball card, others may want to be the classroom monitor, or to get the milk, while still others may want to be captain of the recess team. Your responding skills will help you determine just what your learners consider a privilege and what they consider a punishment.

Examining the Skills of Teaching Delivery 6

You have followed Maria through her preparation for teaching. You have observed segments of her teaching delivery. Reading about what she has done may remind you of your own teaching experiences or give you insights into the profession. When you teach, you plan content and methods for the learners to learn. As they learn, you use their reactions to adjust and alter the content and methods. You do this to facilitate the learners' acquisition of the new learning. And yet, you should ask yourself if you really understand the teaching delivery skills. You may include some of the effective ingredients of teaching delivery, but not all. Use the following models to explore your own teaching delivery skills.

PHASES OF LEARNING

Learning to Explore, Understand, and Act

There are three phases of learning. The first phase is **exploring** the new learning. As you read this material, you are exploring where you are in relation to teaching delivery skills. Taking into consideration what you already know about teaching delivery, you are exploring what else you need to learn. Having determined what you know, the next phase is **understanding** what you need to know. When you explore the skills of teaching delivery, you will understand more fully the function of the new skills. You understand how the new pieces fit with the old pieces so that you are ready for the third phase of learning: **acting**. When you **explore** what you know and **understand** what you need to know, then you can **act** to deliver that knowledge and understanding.

PHASES OF LEARNING

	I EXPLORING	➤	II UNDERSTANDING	➤	III ACTING
Learning Skills	what you know		what you need to know		with what you have learned

Helping Your Learners to Explore, Understand, and Act

Your learners can be effectively taught when you help them **explore** the new learning first. You can give them an opportunity to explore what they know and what they do not know about the new learning. As your learners explore, you may hear them say:

"What's this called?"

"What does this do?"

"Is this right?"

In the second phase, you can help your learners **understand** what they do not know. The more the learners understand, the more often you will hear them say:

"This goes here!"

"I see how this works now!"

"I think I can do it!"

Finally, you will help the learners to **act** in the last phase of learning. Then they will begin to say:

"I can do that!"

"It's my turn!"

"Look at mine!"

Helping your learners to **explore, understand,** and **act** will maximize your success in teaching and your learners' success with learning.

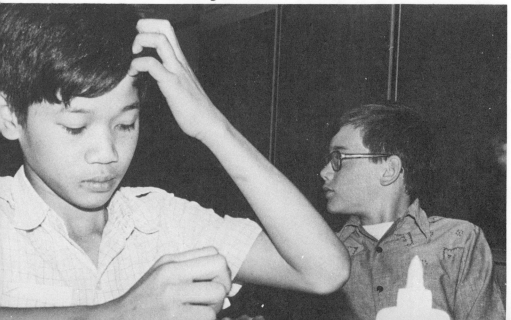

If your students explore, understand and act, then they will learn what you teach.

DELIVER YOUR LESSON WITH ROPES
AND TELL-SHOW-DO-REPEAT-APPLY

ROPES helps you organize your content so that the learners can explore, understand, and act in sequential order. Once the content is arranged in sequence, you employ your methodological skills. You have learned that you **tell, show, do** each section of ROPES. Telling helps your auditory learners and showing helps your visual learners. All of your learners learn more efficiently by doing the learning. In addition to **tell, show, do** methods, you use **repeat** and **apply** methods for the learners' exercise. Content development skills and methodological skills are the foundations of learning in your classroom.

The purpose of teaching is to have students **explore** and **understand** new learning so that they can **act** with that learning. The teacher's preparation and delivery skills are directed to these ends. Before the learners explore the new learning, they should review the contingent skills they have already learned. Since the content is in sequential order from the course title through the daily skills, the previous day's skill will probably be a contingent skill. This allows the teacher to determine where the learners are in relation to previous learning. The teacher plans **tell, show, do** methods to teach these contingency skills.

Content   **Review**
                 ▽
Methods   **Tell**
                 Show
                 Do

Learning   **Exploring**   ▶   **Understanding**   ▶   **Acting**
Skills

Overviewing with Tell-Show-Do

When the learners explore, they examine what they already know about the new skills. They watch how the teacher uses the skills so that they can explore more fully. Much of the learners' exploration occurs in the overview of the lesson. That is the time when the teacher overviews the use of the new skill. Again the teacher selects **tell, show, do** methods which introduce the new learning to the students.

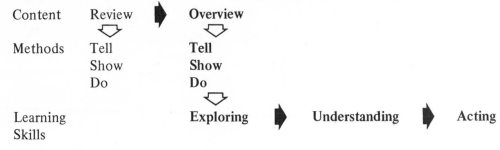

The learners begin to understand the new skill during the presentation. The teacher plans methods which tell the skill steps to the learners. They hear or read what they have to do in order to perform the skill. To add to their understanding, the teacher will plan methods which show the skill steps. Then the teacher plans the most critical aspect for the learners' understanding, the **do** method. The learners are given an opportunity to perform the skill steps themselves. If they understand, they are ready to act with the new skill. If not, then they must go back to relearn the steps, or the teacher may need to add any missing steps.

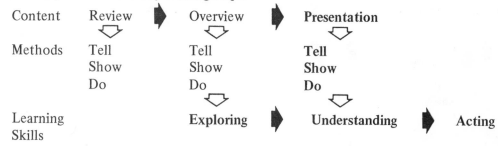

Content	Review	→	Overview	→	**Presentation**
Methods	Tell		Tell		**Tell**
	Show		Show		**Show**
	Do		Do		**Do**
Learning Skills			**Exploring**	→	**Understanding**	→	Acting

Exercising with Repeat-Apply

In the last phase of learning, the teacher plans the exercise for the learners. The exercise should provide the learners with an opportunity to repeat the new skill several times. Once the learners have demonstrated their mastery of the new skill, then they should practice applying the skill. The applications give the learners a chance to use the new skill in conjunction with previously learned skills. The exercise or acting phase of learning should use the majority of class time. Within this phase, the learners will again explore, understand, and act as they apply the new learning.

Before the lesson is over, the teacher will summarize what the learners have learned by **telling**, **showing**, and **doing** the skill steps once more.

Content	Review	▶	Overview	▶	Presentation	▶	Exercise
Methods	Tell Show Do		Tell Show Do		Tell Show Do		**Repeat Apply**
Learning Skills			**Exploring**	▶	**Understanding**	▶	Acting

Before the lesson is over, the teacher will summarize what the learners have learned by **telling**, **showing**, and having them **do** the skill steps once more.

As you can see below, the content in ROPES combines with the methods of Tell-Show-Do-Repeat-Apply to create learner Exploration, Understanding, and Action.

Content	Review	▶	Overview	▶	Presentation	▶	Exercise	▶	**Summary**
Methods	Tell Show Do		Tell Show Do		Tell Show Do		Repeat Apply		**Tell Show Do**
Learning Skills			**Exploring**	▶	**Understanding**	▶	**Acting**		

THE INTERPERSONAL MODEL
OF TEACHING DELIVERY

Diagnosing and Responding Lead to Exploration

There is another dimension that occurs simultaneously with ROPES in the classroom. While the learners are exploring the new learning, the teacher will be exploring, understanding, and acting with the learners' reactions to the learning. The new learning is not created without input from the learners. The most perfectly planned lesson can be an absolute disaster if the teacher ignores the learners' reactions during the delivery.

When the teacher explores with the learners, he or she will respond by diagnosing what the learners know and what they do not know. First the teacher responds to the learners' content, then to the learners' feelings, and finally to their feeling and meaning.

Teacher:	Delivery Skills:	**Diagnosing**
		+
	Interpersonal Skills:	**Responding**
		▽
Learner:	Learning Skills:	**Exploring**

Setting Goals and Personalizing
Lead to Understanding

In the understanding phase of delivery, the teacher uses the diagnosis to set goals for the learners. These goals are directed toward the learners' success with the new learning. The goal may be to learn how to do a missing skill or skill step. Others may need to learn facts, concepts, or principles which are preventing them from completing the skill successfully. The teacher uses personalizing skills when setting goals for the learners. First he or she may personalize the learners' meaning, then their problem, and finally their feelings. Then the teacher can set the learning goals for these learners.

Teacher:	Delivery Skills:	Diagnosing	▶	**Setting Goals**
		+		+
	Interpersonal Skills:	Responding		**Personalizing**
		▽		
Learner:	Learning Skills:	**Exploring**	▶	**Understanding**

Reinforcing and Initiating Lead to Acting

The teacher's action phase of delivery occurs when the learners' behaviors are reinforced. If the learners are moving toward the goal, the teacher will want to give them positive reinforcement. Positive reinforcement encourages the leaders to keep moving towards their goals. When the learners' behavior indicates that they are moving away from the learning goal, the teacher uses negative reinforcement. Neutral reinforcement occurs only when the teacher cannot determine in what direction the learners' behavior is moving.

Teacher:	Delivery Skills:	Diagnosing	➤	Setting Goals	➤	Reinforcing
		+		+		+
	Interpersonal Skills:	Responding		Personalizing		Initiating
		⬇		⬇		⬇
Learner:	Learning Skills:	Exploring	➤	Understanding	➤	Acting

PUTTING IT ALL TOGETHER

These are the models for the teacher and the learner. They reduce the complexity of teaching delivery to the essential skills. It is the interaction of these skills that complicate teaching delivery. How you choose to use these skills will determine your effectiveness as a teacher.

Glimpse once more into Maria's classroom. She uses all of the teaching delivery skills effectively in a forty-five minute class. It may be important for you to identify these skills and the frequency with which these skills are used. Then you can understand what makes a delivery effective.

The classroom windows rattled and shook as the first winter storm began. Sleet struck the windows in waves, filling the classroom with its clatter. Maria brought her students over to the windows to view the storm better. A swirl of snowflakes swept past, followed by a wave of sleet.

"Is it gonna rain or snow, Miss Burbank?" asked John.

"I hope it's going to snow," said Patrice.

"Yeah," added Tony. "Then we can have a snowball fight on the way."

"Let's look at the temperature first," said Maria. "Kenneth, can you read the temperature for us?"

Craning his neck, Kenneth squinted at the thermometer, just outside the window. "It says 34 degrees . . . no . . . it's 1 degree," he said, obviously confused.

"You're right — both times. The first is Fahrenheit, the other is centigrade. Write them both on the board, will you, and the time we took the temperature." Marie turned to Janet. "Can you tell us at what temperature water freezes, Janet — by either scale?"

Janet blinked her eyes several times nervously. "Uh . . . Uh . . . don't give me the answer . . . I know it!" Her face broke into a broad grin. "It's 32 degrees Fahrenheit."

"You're absolutely correct, Janet. Water freezes at 32 degrees Fahrenheit." Maria continued to explain to her students how the temperature would have to stay at the freezing level in order for the snow to accumulate.

Maria looked at the twenty-five faces of her students. She felt herself catching their excitement about the weather as they chatted about other winter storms they had known. Smiling to herself she took in their varied expressions. It had been nearly three months since she began teaching these kids. Maria had learned a lot about them and they were learning a lot from her.

"Let's have a contest," suggested Maria, "to see who can guess how much snow we're going to have." She herded the children back to their seats where they wrote their guesses down on slips of paper. Angela walked around collecting all the slips in an empty shoebox.

"I know how excited you all feel about the storm. You have so much fun when it snows." Maria responded to her class's feelings. "But now we've got to get busy with the math lesson." A resigned sigh rose up from the class. "Besides," she added, "before we're finished today, we'll have our own snowstorm right inside our class." With that, the students all sat a little straighter in their seats and focused their attention on Maria.

She began the math class with a review of compass skills. "Why do we use a compass?" Several hands shot up. "Yes, Kenneth?"

"It helps you draw circles real good."

"Good, Kenneth. You're saying that compasses make accurate circles." Maria continued with her review. She had Theresa tell the others the steps of drawing a circle with the compass, while Tony showed the steps on the chalkboard with a giant wooden compass that held chalk. Then Maria had all the students draw some circles with their compasses. Next she reviewed how to divide the circumference of the circle into sixths by using the radius of the circle. This time, Janet described the principle of "pi" while she told and showed the class how to divide the circumference. Everyone practiced on the circles they had previously drawn. Maria made a quick survey of all the students' work. Then she knew they were ready to move on.

Maria began the overview by telling the class that a circle has 360 degrees. She wrote 360 in large numerals on the chalkboard and drew a circle next to it. Then she asked if anyone knew how many degrees there were in a square corner. Finally she took out a large wooden protractor and explained its function. She drew three different angles on the chalkboard and then had the class write down what they guessed the measures of each to be.

Manny raised his hand. "It's easy to tell that that one's 90 degrees." He pointed to the right angle on the board. "But I can't tell how big the other two are."

"You're saying that you need a way to measure these other angles. You need the protractor." With that, she measured each angle with her protractor and wrote their measure down beneath each angle.

"I didn't see. What did you do?" called out Kenneth anxiously.

"You want to learn how to use the protractor, Kenneth. Let me show you the steps." Maria was ready to teach her lesson.

Maria went over to her supply closet and brought out a box of plastic protractors. "Pass these out, John," she said as she handed him the box.

Happily, John jumped up, glad for an excuse to move around. Maria smiled, for she knew he had a hard time staying quiet in his seat for any length of time. She started counting out freshly dittoed worksheets to the groups of students seated around the room.

"Hey, cut that out, Manny!" threatened John. Maria directed her attention toward Manny and John. She watched as Manny tried to grab the box of protractors from John. Holding his ground against the larger boy, John kept insisting that Manny already had his protractor.

Maria made her decision to intercede. Walking over to Manny she said, "It's wrong for you to keep the class waiting, Manny. All the protractors are the same and John has given you one already. Maria looked sharply at Manny who hung his head, avoiding Maria's gaze. Satisfied with his reaction, she did not feel that she had to add any more to the negative reinforcement she had given. She walked to the front of the class and wrote the first skill step on the chalkboard.

She then showed them the steps she had written on the chalkboard, while the students followed along with her. Everyone seemed to understand how to use the protractor to measure angles. Next, Maria wrote the steps to making a measured angle with the protractor. Again she demonstrated with a yardstick and the protractor on the board. Then she circulated around the room while the students practiced making angles with their protractors.

Janet stopped Maria as she passed her desk. "I can't tell what I'm doing wrong, Miss Burbank. But I can't do this at all."

"You're mixed-up, Janet, because you don't know what you're doing wrong. Why don't you show me how you do the steps." Maria watched as Janet struggled to make an angle. "I see your problem, Janet. You're reading the bottom scale. Here," Maria indicated the two rows of numbers around the protractor. "Start with the zero on the left and work your way around until you come to 75."

"Oh, I see," said Janet with relief. "I have to start with zero and go up. Just like counting. I can do it now!"

"It feels good to be able to do your work well, Janet."

"Now we're ready to make our own snowstorm," Maria told the class. "And speaking of snowstorms . . . " She motioned toward the windows. The children looked and cheered. Giant snowflakes floated by outside the windows. The streets were covered here and there with patches of white. "Patrice, you read the temperature this time."

Patrice scrambled out of her seat and studied the outdoor thermometer. Turning to the class, her eyes sparkling, she announced the temperature to be 31 degrees. Again the classroom filled with sounds of the children's approval.

Maria could not hide the enthusiasm she had caught from her students. "I wonder who will win the contest."

"ME!" shouted each and every student.

Maria was ready for the exercise of her lesson. "While I pass out the materials for our snowstorm I want you to finish the worksheet I handed out." This was the repeat exercise which had the students measure several angles on the worksheet and then make some specific angles, all with their protractors. Maria laid out white paper, string, and scissors at the long table in the back of the room.

Examining each student's worksheet, she moved around correcting what they had done. "You really understand how to use the protractors," she told the class. "Now you can use your compasses and protractors to make snowflakes."

Maria explained the symmetry of snowflakes and then she gave the directions using the overhead projector. The classroom came alive as students moved to collect the materials they needed.

"I don't think I can do this, Miss Burbank," sighed Janet with a doomed-to-failure attitude.

"Theresa, will you come and work with Janet?" The idea of help from one of the "brains" reassured Janet and once again she looked happy.

Making her rounds, Maria stopped beside Kenneth's desk. He looked so dejected that Maria pulled up a chair beside him.

"You feel pretty down today, Kenneth," responded Maria.

Avoiding her gaze, he nodded his head up and down.

"Is it the work that's making you feel so bad?"

He shook his head back and forth this time. "Nope! It's just that Mr. Abbott's gonna be awful mad at me." The words, once started, tumbled from his mouth in a jumble.

"I was supposed to bring in an absence note. What a dumb thing! Who needs them anyhow. So what if I forgot? Maybe I'll never bring it in!"

Maria responded to his feelings and meaning. "You feel down because Mr. Abbott is going to get angry with you."

"Yeah, he's gonna make me stay after and I won't get a chance to snowball fight with the guys. He'll ruin it all."

"You're upset because you won't be able to have fun because you forgot your note."

"Naw, I didn't forget it. My Ma left for work this morning before I got up. She forgot! I told her last night. She forgot!"

"It makes you angry because your mother forgot to write the note." Maria was exploring with Kenneth, trying to diagnose what his problem was.

"Yeah, she forgot, not me!"

At this point Maria was ready to personalize. "You're upset because you don't think you will be able to explain this to Mr. Abbott so that he will understand."

For the first time, Kenneth looked directly at Maria. His brow furrowed as he fought back tears of frustration. "How can I tell him so he won't get mad at me?"

At this point, Maria could help Kenneth with his problem. He nad a goal. He wanted to be able to explain his problem to Mr. Abbott in such a way that he wouldn't get detention. Together they rehearsed what Kenneth would say to Mr. Abbott. Then, as a first step, Maria wrote a note for him to carry to the office, simply stating that Kenneth had something important to explain.

Turning her attention back to the rest of the class, she moved on to Tony's desk. A stack of four snowflakes attested to his skill with the compass and protractor.

"Tony, these are really great snowflakes. How would you like to use your compass and protractor to make some three-dimensional models?"

Tony's eyes lit up. "Ya mean like real crystals?" he asked. Maria nodded her head.

She found a pamphlet in her file on constructions. "This icosahedron should be fun for you to make."

Maria paused and looked around. "I better get to the others," she thought. "One thing you can say about teaching . . . there's never a dull moment!"

Mr. Abbott appeared in the doorway with Kenneth, one arm around his shoulders. Maria thought with relief, "He did it!" She flashed Kenneth a triumphant smile and he responded with an A-OK signal. Going over to the door she spoke. "Come on in and see **our** snowstorm, Mr. Abbott. I know it looks busy! Everyone is working hard on applying their compass and protractor skills."

The principal's visit had a focusing effect on the class, who set to work with much more vigor. "See mine, Mr. Abbott," said Janet proudly as she held her completed snowflake up to be admired.

"That's really good, Janet. I can tell you measured correctly because your flake is even on all sides. Would you make me one for my office?"

"Sure will, Mr. Abbott. Theresa helped me do it so good."

"Maybe someday, Theresa, you'll be a teacher. It looks like you'd make a good one!"

Theresa blushed with the attention she was getting from the principal. Softly she replied, "Someday I'd like to be a teacher . . . just like Miss Burbank."

REFERENCES

1. Developing yearly content. See Chapter 2 of **The Skills of Teaching: Content Development Skills.** Amherst, Mass.: Human Resource Development Press, 1978.

2. Developing daily content. See Chapters 3 and 4 of **The Skills of Teaching: Content Development Skills.**

3. Organizing the content of a lesson plan. See Chapter 2 of **The Skills of Teaching: Lesson Planning Skills.** Amherst, Mass.: Human Resource Development Press, 1978.

4. Planning the methods of a lesson plan. See Chapters 3, 4, and 5 of **The Skills of Teaching: Lesson Planning Skills.**

5. Attending skills. See Chapter 3 of **The Skills of Teaching: Interpersonal Skills,** Amherst, Mass.: Human Resource Development Press, 1977.

6. Responding to content. See Chapter 3, Page 75, of **The Skills of Teaching: Interpersonal Skills.**

7. Responding to feelings. See Chapter 4 of **The Skills of Teaching: Interpersonal Skills.**

8. Responding to feeling and meaning. See Chapter 4 of **The Skills of Teaching: Interpersonal Skills.**

9. Personalizing meaning. See Chapter 5 of **The Skills of Teaching: Interpersonal Skills.**

10. Personalizing feelings. See Chapter 5 of **The Skills of Teaching: Interpersonal Skills.**

11. Personalizing problems and goals. See Chapter 5 of **The Skills of Teaching: Interpersonal Skills.**

BIBLIOGRAPHY

Aspy, D.N.
Toward a Technology for Humanizing Education
Champaign, Illinois: Research Press, 1972
Useful for understanding the research base for the facilitative interpersonal dimensions of the Carkhuff Model in education. Contains introductions to Flanders Interaction Analysis and Bloom's cognitive processes as well as empathy, congruence and regard. Concludes that teachers with high levels of interpersonal skills have students who achieve more.

Aspy, D.N. and Roebuck, F.N.
Kids Don't Learn from People They Don't Like
Amherst, Massachusetts: Human Resource Development Press, 1977.
Useful for understanding the research base for the Carkhuff Model in teaching. Studies the differential effects of training in Flanders, Bloom and Carkhuff skills. Hundreds of teachers were trained. The effects on thousands of learners were studied. Significant gains were achieved on the following indices: student absenteeism and tardiness; student discipline and school crises; student learning skills and cognitive growth. Concludes that the Carkhuff model is the preferred teacher training model.

Berenson, B.G.
Belly-to-Belly and Back-to-Back: The Militant Humanism of Robert R. Carkhuff
Amherst, Massachusetts: Human Resource Development Press, 1975.
Useful for an understanding of the human assumptions underlying the human and educational resource development models of Carkhuff. Presents a collection of prose and poetry by Carkhuff. Concludes by challenging us to die growing.

Berenson, B.G. and Carkhuff, R.R.
The Sources of Gain in Counseling and Psychotherapy
New York: Holt, Rinehart and Winston, 1967.
Useful for an in-depth view of the different orientations to helping. Integrates the research of diverse approaches to helping. Concludes with a model of core conditions around which the different preferred modes of treatment make their own unique contributions to helpee benefits.

Berenson, B.G. and Mitchell, K.M.
Confrontation: For Better or Worse
Amherst, Massachusetts: Human Resource Development Press, 1974.
Useful for an in-depth view of confrontation and immediacy as well as the core interpersonal dimensions. Presents extensive experimental manipulation of core interpersonal skills and confrontation and immediacy. Concludes that while confrontation is never necessary and never sufficient, in the hands of an effective helper, it may be efficient for moving the helpee toward constructive gain or change.

Berenson, D.H., S.R. Berenson and Carkhuff, R.R.
The Skills of Teaching— Content Development Skills
Amherst, Massachusetts: Human Resource Development Press, in press, 1978.
Useful for learning skills needed for developing teaching content. Develops skills based content in terms of **do** and **think** steps and supportive knowledge in terms of facts, concepts and principles. Concludes that content must be developed programmatically in order to insure teaching delivery.

Berenson, S.R.; Carkhuff, R.R.; Berenson, D.H. and Pierce, R.M.

The Do's and Don'ts of Teaching
Amherst, Massachusetts: Human Resource Development Press, 1977.

Useful for pre-service and in-service teachers. Lays out the interpersonal skills of teaching and their effect in the most basic form. Concludes that effective teachers apply skills that facilitate their learners' involvement in learning.

Carkhuff, R.R.

Helping and Human Relations.
Vol. I. Selection and Training
Vol. 2. Practice and Research
New York: Holt, Rinehart and Winston, 1969.

Useful for understanding the research base for interpersonal skills in counseling and education. Operationalizes the helping process in great detail. Presents extensive research evidence for systematic selection, training and treatment procedures. Concludes that teaching is the preferred mode of treatment for helping.

Carkhuff, R.R.

The Development of Human Resources:
Education, Psychology and Social Change
New York: Holt, Rinehart and Winston, 1971.

Useful for understanding applications of human resource development (HRD) models. Describes and presents research evidence for numerous applications in helping skills training in human, educational and community resource development. Concludes that systematic planning for human delivery systems can be effectively translated into human benefits.

Carkhuff, R.R.

The Art of Helping III
Amherst, Massachusetts: Human Resource Development Press, 3rd Edition, 1977

Useful for learning helping skills. Includes attending, responding, personalizing and initiating modules. Concludes that helping is a way of life.

Carkhuff, R.R. and Berenson, B.G.
Beyond Counseling and Therapy
New York: Holt, Rinehart and Winston, 2nd Edition, 1977.

Useful for understanding of the core interpersonal conditions and their implications and applications. Adds many core dimensions and factors them out as responsive and initiative dimensions. Includes an analysis of the client-centered, existential, psychoanalytic, trait-and-factor and behavioristic orientations to helping. Concludes that only the trait-and-factor and behavioristic positions make unique contributions to human benefits over and above the core conditions.

Carkhuff, R.R. and Berenson, B.G.
Teaching As Treatment
Amherst, Massachusetts: Human Resource Development Press, 1976.

Useful for understanding the development of a human technology. Operationalizes the helping process as teaching. Offers research evidence for living, learning and working skills development and physical, emotional and intellectual outcomes. Concludes that learning-to-learn is the fundamental model for living, learning and working.

Carkhuff, R.R.; Berenson, D.H. and
Berenson, S.R.
The Skills of Teaching—
Lesson Planning Skills
Amherst, Massachusetts: Human
Resource Development Press, in press,
1978.
> Useful for learning skills needed to
> prepare for delivering content.
> Organizes lessons by reviewing,
> overviewing, presenting, exercising
> and summarizing. Breaks the
> organization down into a tell-show-
> do format. Concludes that content
> must be delivered in programmatic
> ways in order to maximize learning.

Carkhuff, R.R.; Devine, J.; Berenson, B.G.;
Griffin, A.H.; Angelone, R.; Keeling, T.;
Patch, W. and Steinberg, H.
Cry Twice!
Amherst, Massachusetts: Human
Resource Development Press, 1973.
> Useful for understanding the
> ingredients of institutional change.
> Details the people, programs and
> organizational variables needed to
> transform an institution from a
> custodial to a treatment orientation.
> Concludes that institutional change
> begins with people change.

Carkhuff, R.R and Pierce, R.M.
Teacher As Person
Washington, D.C.: National Education
Association, 1976.
> Useful for teachers interested in
> ameliorating the effects of sexism and
> racism. Includes modules and ap-
> plications of interpersonal skills in the
> school. Concludes that behaviors
> teachers practice influence learning
> students accomplish.

Rogers, C.R.; Gendlin, E.T.; Kiesler, D.
and Truax, C.B.
The Therapeutic Relationship and
Its Impact
Madison, Wisconsin: University of
Wisconsin Press, 1967.
> Useful for understanding the
> transitional phases in developing
> HRD models. Presents extensive
> evidence on training lay and
> professional helpers as well as dif-
> ferent orientations to helping.
> Concludes that the core interpersonal
> dimensions of empathy, respect and
> genuineness are critical to effective
> helping.

Truax, C.B. and Carkhuff, R.R.
Toward Effective Counseling
and Therapy
Chicago, Illinois: Aldine, 1967.
> Useful for understanding the
> historical roots of the HRD models.
> Presents extensive evidence on client-
> centered counseling for schizophrenic
> patients. Concludes that core in-
> terpersonal dimensions of empathy,
> regard and congruence are critical to
> effective helping.

DATE DUE			

GAYLORD   PRINTED IN U.S A.